TEACH
THE
BRAIN

TEACH THE BRAIN

Neuroscience Tools For Educators To
Empower Learning And Growth

SACHA S. G. CORNUAULT

Title: Teach the Brain: Neuroscience Tools for Educators to Empower Learning and Growth

Author: Sacha S. G. Cornuault Publisher: Mindset Publishing LLC

Subject: Education | Neuroscience | Cognitive Science | Learning & Development

Cover Design by Claire Woodfield

Illustrations by Sacha S. G. Cornuault

ISBN (Paperback): 978-1-7640093-1-7 | For permission or enquiries, contact: mindsetpublishingllc@gmail.com

For Claire, Emma, Mickael, and Julianna - your support, wisdom, and encouragement have shaped this journey.

This book is for you.

"The beautiful thing about learning is that no one can take it away from you."

— B.B. King

CONTENTS

INTRODUCTION

What if you could unlock the full potential of your students by understanding how their brains work? In every classroom, training session, or coaching interaction, the human brain is at the center of learning. Yet, many teaching practices rely on tradition rather than the growing body of research on how the brain processes, retains, and applies information. *Teach the Brain: Neuroscience Tools for Educators to Empower Learning and Growth* bridges this gap, offering practical, research-based strategies to enhance learning outcomes and student engagement.

This book equips educators, coaches, and facilitators with actionable tools rooted in neuroscience to address key challenges in modern education. From improving memory retention with strategies like spaced repetition and active recall to leveraging the brain's reward system for motivation, the methods outlined here are designed to work in real-world settings. These approaches have the power to not only improve academic performance, but can also facilitate environments where learners feel supported, valued, and empowered.

Understanding the science of learning also means addressing the emotional and social dimensions of education. This book highlights how mindfulness practices, emotional regulation techniques, and gratitude exercises can reduce stress and improve focus for both educators and learners. Additionally, it provides practical ways to promote inclusivity, foster a growth mindset, and tailor lessons to diverse needs, ensuring every student has the opportunity to succeed.

Whether you are teaching in a classroom, mentoring individuals, or leading professional development, *Teach the Brain* delivers the tools and insights needed to transform your approach to education. By grounding strategies in how the brain learns best, this resource will help you create lasting, meaningful learning experiences for all your students.

1

Understanding the Brain and Learning

The neuroscience of learning examines how the brain processes, retains, and retrieves information. By understanding these mechanisms, educators can develop strategies that enhance learning outcomes and student engagement. Rather than relying solely on traditional teaching methods, educators who apply neuroscience insights can create environments where teaching aligns with how the brain naturally operates.

One key concept in brain-based learning is neuroplasticity, the brain's ability to adapt and form new neural connections. This adaptability means that experiences can reshape how we think and learn. Active learning strategies, such as problem-solving and collaborative projects, stimulate the brain to form and strengthen neural pathways. These activities promote deeper cognitive engagement, leading to improved comprehension and retention.

Memory is another critical factor in learning. Techniques like spaced repetition, which involves reviewing information at specific intervals, leverage the brain's natural forgetting process to strengthen recall over time. This method helps reinforce knowledge, reduce cognitive overload, and improve long-term retention. Similarly, strategies such as retrieval practice—actively recalling information rather than simply reviewing it—can further enhance memory. Emotions also play a significant role in learning. The amygdala, which processes emotions, works closely with the hippocampus, the brain's memory center. When students form emotional connections to content—such as through storytelling or real-world applications—they are more likely to retain that information. Incorporating narratives into lessons can make material more engaging and memorable. Finally, motivation is essential for effective learning. The brain's reward system, which involves the release of dopamine during rewarding experiences, drives persistence and effort. Educators can tap into this system by setting achievable goals and providing positive reinforcement when students meet them. This approach increases motivation and fosters a growth mindset, where challenges are seen as opportunities for improvement.

By integrating these neuroscience insights—neuroplasticity, memory techniques, emotional connections, and motivation, educators can create enriched learning experiences that support student success and personal growth.

Memory systems, particularly working memory and long-term memory are central to the learning process. Working memory allows students to temporarily hold and manipulate information, which is critical for problem solving and following multi-step instructions. Educators can support this by breaking complex information into smaller, more manageable chunks or incorporating visual aids that engage multiple senses to reinforce learning. Social cognition, which is the ability to understand and navigate social interactions and emotions, plays a significant role in education. Collaborative learning environments encourage peer interaction, communication, and teamwork, enhancing both social and academic skills. Group activities, such as project-based learning and classroom discussions, foster empathy, cooperation, and the ability to work effectively with others—skills that are essential for future success. Understanding and leveraging these key brain functions—executive function, attention, memory systems, and social cognition—can help educators create targeted strategies to enhance learning experiences. By aligning teaching methods with how the brain naturally operates, educators can promote an environment where students are better equipped to succeed.

Implications for Teaching Practices

Understanding how brain functions influence teaching practices is essential for improving student learning outcomes. By aligning instructional strategies with how the brain processes information, educators can create effective and engaging learning environments. This alignment not only supports cognitive development but also encourages emotional and social growth.

One key implication is the importance of **differentiated instruction**, which accommodates diverse learning styles and paces. Since each student's brain processes information uniquely, teachers can use a variety of methods, such as visual aids, hands-on activities, and group work, to address individual needs. For example, incorporating multimedia resources can engage visual learners, while group discussions provide opportunities for social learners to thrive. These strategies ensure that students connect with material in ways that resonate with them, promoting both engagement and deeper understanding of the task or concept at hand.

Another critical aspect is fostering executive function skills through structured routines and explicit instruction. Teachers can use tools like checklists or time management activities to help students organize and plan their work. Embedding these strategies into the curriculum can equip students with the self-regulation skills needed to manage their learning effectively and perform better academically.

The role of attention in learning highlights the need to design environments that support sustained focus. Techniques such as short breaks, mindfulness exercises, and alternating activities can help students maintain concentration. For instance, participation in a brief mindfulness activity before a challenging lesson can help students reset and prepare for focused work. These strategies improve attention and enhance the overall retention of information.

Finally, promoting social cognition through collaborative learning experiences is essential for building interpersonal skills. Activities like group projects and peer tutoring encourage students to share knowledge while developing empathy, communication, and teamwork abilities. These skills are valuable for academic success and critical for personal and professional growth.

Aligning teaching practices with brain functions—through differentiated instruction, executive function development, attention strategies, and social cognition activities—enables educators to create environments where students can thrive academically, socially, and emotionally.

2

MEMORY RETENTION TECHNIQUES

What if your students could remember more of what they learn and recall it when it matters most? This chapter focuses on three proven strategies—spaced repetition, storytelling, and active recall—that align with how the brain processes and stores information. By applying these methods, educators can support students in achieving deeper understanding and long-term retention, equipping them for sustained success.

Spaced Repetition Strategies

Spaced repetition is an evidence-based learning technique that enhances memory retention by leveraging the brain's natural forgetting curve. By systematically timing the review of material, this method helps learners retain knowledge over longer periods.

In educational settings, spaced repetition offers a practical solution for promoting deeper understanding and moving beyond short-term memorization.

The principle behind spaced repetition is simple: revisit learned material at progressively longer intervals. For example, after initially studying a concept, a student might review it the following day, then three days later, then a week after that, and so on. This systematic review process strengthens memory by facilitating the transfer of information from short-term to long-term memory storage. Studies consistently show that spaced repetition improves retention compared to traditional cramming methods.

Digital tools, such as Anki and Quizlet, provide effective platforms for implementing spaced repetition. These systems use algorithms to determine the optimal review schedule based on a learner's progress and familiarity with the material. By focusing on areas of difficulty and reducing time spent on mastered content, these tools maximize efficiency and improve learning outcomes.

Spaced repetition can also be integrated into classroom instruction to benefit both educators and students. Teachers can design curricula that include periodic reviews of key concepts throughout a course, rather than concentrating assessments at the end of units. This approach reinforces memory and allows students to connect new material with prior knowledge, fostering deeper understanding and application.

Beyond cognitive advantages, spaced repetition encourages the development of a growth mindset. As students experience repeated success in recalling information, they gain confidence in their learning abilities and become more resilient when faced with challenges. By embedding spaced repetition into educational practices, educators empower students to take ownership of their learning, improve retention, and achieve sustained academic success.

The Power of Storytelling

Storytelling is a powerful educational tool that enhances memory retention and promotes cognitive engagement. By presenting information in the form of narratives, educators can help learners create mental frameworks that improve understanding and recall. Stories align with the brain's natural preference for structured, relatable content, making complex ideas more accessible and memorable.

The strength of storytelling lies in its ability to evoke emotions and create vivid mental images. When information is tied to a narrative, it becomes anchored in emotional experiences, which are inherently more memorable than isolated facts. For example, teaching historical events through the experiences of individuals who lived during those times humanizes the material and also helps students form personal connections to the content. Storytelling aids comprehension by providing context and structure. Narratives can illustrate cause-and-effect relationships, emphasize key themes, and present challenges and resolutions, making abstract or complex ideas easier to grasp. In classrooms, educators can frame lessons within central narratives that guide students through the learning process and help them retain key concepts.

Practical applications of storytelling in education vary widely. In business education, case studies provide real-world examples that contextualize theoretical principles. In medical training, simulated patient histories help students apply their knowledge in realistic scenarios. These approaches improve retention and prepare students to apply what they learn in practical settings.

Advancements in digital technology have further enhanced storytelling's role in education. Tools such as podcasts and videos enables learners to engage with narratives interactively. These formats promote active participation and allow students to explore content at their own pace, making learning more engaging and personalized.

By integrating storytelling into teaching practices, educators can transform the passive consumption of information into an interactive and meaningful learning experience. This approach helps students remember facts and internalize knowledge in a way that is lasting and applicable beyond the classroom.

Active Recall Methods

Active recall is a highly effective learning strategy that focuses on retrieving information from memory rather than passively reviewing material. This approach is widely supported in educational psychology for its ability to enhance long-term retention and deepen understanding. By actively engaging with content, learners strengthen the neural pathways associated with the information, making it more accessible over time.

A common and effective form of active recall is the use of flashcards. Flashcards prompt learners to recall answers based on questions or keywords, facilitating repeated retrieval practice. This process has been shown to significantly improve memory retention compared to passive review methods. The digital tools mentioned earlier, Anki and Quizlet, can also be used to enhance this technique by using spaced repetition algorithms, which optimize review schedules for maximum efficiency.

Another active recall strategy is self-quizzing or practice testing. This can include answering questions at the end of textbook chapters or completing online quizzes related to the material. Research shows that practice testing reinforces knowledge and helps learners identify areas that require further review, enabling more focused and efficient study.

Teaching others, often referred to as the **Feynman Technique**, is another effective method of active recall. By explaining a concept in simple terms to someone else, learners are forced to clarify their understanding and address any gaps in their knowledge. This process reinforces memory while enhancing comprehension through the act of articulation.

Incorporating active recall into daily routines can further improve learning outcomes. For example, students might summarize what they've learned at the end of a lesson or create **mind maps** to visually connect related concepts. These practices encourage continuous engagement and deeper processing of information.

Active recall transforms learning into an interactive process that promotes critical thinking and long-term retention. Educators can empower students to take a more active role in their learning and achieve greater academic success by integrating these methods into educational practice.

3

MOTIVATION AND THE BRAIN

Motivation plays a central role in driving student engagement, persistence, and success. In this chapter, we explore how the brain's reward system influences learning and examine strategies such as goal-setting, positive reinforcement, and relevance-driven teaching to sustain motivation. By understanding the neuroscience behind motivation, educators can create environments that inspire students to approach challenges with confidence and maintain focus on their learning goals.

The brain's reward system involves several key structures, including the **ventral tegmental area (VTA)**, **nucleus accumbens**, and **prefrontal cortex**. These areas work together to process rewards and reinforce behaviors that lead to positive outcomes. When students achieve a goal or receive praise, the brain releases **dopamine**, a neurotransmitter linked to reward and reinforcement. This release generates feelings of satisfaction and strengthens the likelihood of repeating the behavior.

KEY BRAIN STRUCTURES IN REWARD & MOTIVATION

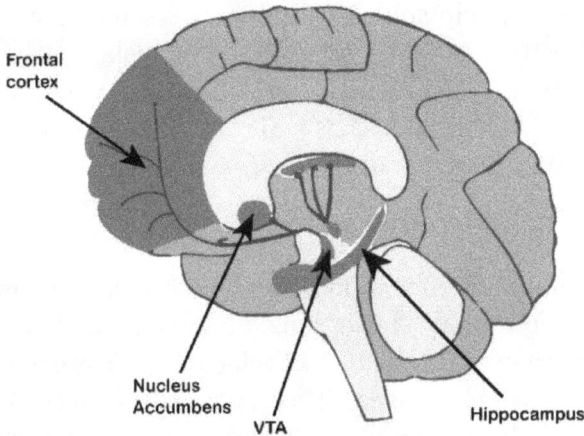

Key Aspects of the Rewards System in Education

The rewards system in education leverages the brain's natural mechanisms, such as dopamine release, to drive motivation and engagement in learning. By understanding and applying strategies such as goal setting and positive reinforcement, educators can create environments that encourage persistence, foster a growth mindset, and improve overall student outcomes.

Dopamine Release

Dopamine plays a key role in reinforcing learning. For example, when a student successfully completes a challenging task, the release of dopamine provides a sense of accomplishment and strengthens their memory of the steps they took to succeed. This process encourages persistence and promotes skill development.

Goal-Setting

Setting meaningful goals, and then making progress toward achieving these goals can effectively activate the reward system. Educators can help students establish personal milestones that align with their interests or aspirations, making achievements more satisfying and motivational. Breaking larger tasks into smaller, attainable steps also allows students to experience frequent successes.

Positive Reinforcement

Recognizing both effort and achievement is a powerful way to enhance motivation. Praise, tangible rewards and constructive feedback can make students feel valued as well as encouraged to take on new challenges. This approach fosters a positive classroom culture where students are willing to engage and take academic risks.

Relevance-Driven Motivation

Connecting lessons to real-world applications boosts intrinsic motivation by helping students see the value of what they are learning. When students understand how their education relates to their lives and future goals, they are more likely to engage deeply and sustain their interest over time.

Goal Setting for Success

Goal-setting is a powerful strategy that significantly influences motivation and achievement. By providing direction and activating the brain's reward system, working towards clear and attainable goals enables learners to stay focused, engaged, and committed to their objectives in educational settings.

The primary benefit of goal-setting is its ability to provide **clarity and purpose**. Specific objectives help students understand what needs to be accomplished and create a framework for tracking progress. This structured approach fosters a sense of ownership over their learning. For example, a student aiming to improve their math skills might set incremental goals such as completing daily practice problems or mastering a specific concept each week.

Effective goal-setting often follows the **SMART criteria**— Specific, Measurable, Achievable, Relevant, and Time-bound. This ensures that goals are realistic and actionable, increasing the likelihood of success. For instance, instead of a vague statement like "I want to improve in school," a student could define a goal such as, "I will study for 30 minutes each day after school for the next month." A clear goal like this promotes consistent effort and enables students to evaluate their progress.

S	**SPECIFIC** **What do I want to accomplish?**	Precisely define what you want to achieve • Focus on one clear objective • Answer: Who? What? Where? Why?
M	**MEASURABLE** **How will I know when it is accomplished?**	Establish criteria to track progress • Identify quantifiable indicators or evidence • Answer: How much? How many? How will I know?
A	**ACHIEVABLE** **How can the goal be accomplished?**	Set goals that are challenging but realistic • Ensure you have resources and skills or can acquire them • Answer: Is this goal attainable?
R	**RELEVANT** **Does this seem worthwile?**	Align the goal with broader objectives • Keep it meaningful and connected to purpose • Answer: Why does this matter now?
T	**TIME BOUND** **When can I accomplish this goal?**	Assign a clear deadline or schedule • Specify exact dates or milestones • Answer: By when will I achieve this goal?

While the SMART framework provides a structured approach to goal-setting, it is important to keep its limitations in mind when applying it. A highly rigid goal may leave little room for adaptation, making it challenging for students to adjust their objectives as they learn and grow. Additionally, the emphasis on measurable and time-bound outcomes can sometimes shift focus toward short-term achievements rather than fostering deeper learning and long-term development. Lastly, an overemphasis on reaching specific targets may create unnecessary pressure, reducing intrinsic motivation and discouraging exploration beyond the set objectives. By remaining aware of these limitations, educators and students can use the framework more flexibly, ensuring that goals remain supportive rather than restrictive.

Breaking larger goals into smaller milestones further enhances motivation. Achieving these smaller targets—such as completing an assignment on time or improving a quiz score— provides regular opportunities for positive reinforcement. Each success triggers the release of dopamine, reinforcing effort and encourages continued progress.

Goal-setting is a foundational practice for fostering motivation and success in education. By guiding students to define clear, actionable goals and break them into manageable steps, educators can help create environments that promote engagement and achievement. As students experience progress, they develop the confidence and resilience needed to tackle challenges and reach their full potential.

Positive Reinforcement Techniques

Positive reinforcement is a proven strategy for enhancing motivation and promoting desired behaviors, particularly in educational and behavioral settings. By leveraging the brain's reward system, positive reinforcement encourages learners to repeat behaviors that lead to rewarding outcomes, ultimately fostering better engagement and learning.

The foundation of positive reinforcement lies in its ability to strengthen behavior through rewards. When an individual performs a desired action and receives a positive response, the brain releases dopamine, which creates feelings of satisfaction and reinforces the connection between the behavior and its outcome. For example, when a student completes their homework on time and receives praise from a teacher, they are more likely to maintain this behavior in the future.

Effective Techniques for Positive Reinforcement:

Verbal Praise

Verbal reinforcement, such as acknowledging effort or accomplishments with specific and meaningful feedback, is a simple yet powerful motivator. For example, phrases like "Great job organizing your ideas in this essay" or "I'm impressed by your progress in solving these problems" can boost self-esteem and encourage continued effort.

Tangible Rewards

Stickers, certificates, and small prizes, serve as physical reminders of achievement. These are particularly effective with younger learners, who often respond well to visible and immediate rewards for meeting goals.

Social Recognition

Publicly recognizing achievements—such as showcasing a student's work during class discussions or highlighting accomplishments in school assemblies—can provide a sense of pride and motivate others to strive for similar success.

Gamification

Incorporating elements of gamification into learning activities can serve as a powerful motivator. For example, point systems that allow students to earn points for completing tasks, which can then be exchanged for privileges or rewards, encourage sustained effort and participation.

Tiered Reward Systems

A tiered approach, where smaller rewards lead to larger incentives over time, can help students stay motivated while working toward long-term goals. This structure ensures continuous engagement while promoting persistence and effort.

The timing of reinforcement is critical to its effectiveness. Providing immediate feedback after a desired behavior strengthens the association between the action and its outcome, making it more likely to be repeated. Delayed reinforcement, while still beneficial, may reduce the impact of the reward.

Positive reinforcement techniques are versatile tools that can be tailored to individual needs and preferences. By strategically applying these methods, educators can create a motivating and supportive learning environment that encourages students to remain engaged and take pride in their achievements.

4

RELEVANCE DRIVEN LEARNING

Connecting curriculum to real life can significantly help in fostering student engagement and promoting deeper understanding. When students see the practical applications of what they are learning, they become more motivated to participate actively in their education. This approach enhances the relevance of learning and also prepares students for real-world challenges by equipping them with applicable skills. In this chapter, we discuss the importance of contextual learning, as well as fostering a sense of curiosity and interest.

One effective strategy for bridging the gap between academic content and real- world applications is project-based learning (PBL). This method is a subset of contextual learning, and involves students engaging in projects that require them to solve authentic problems or create tangible products. For example, a science class could collaborate with local environmental organizations to measure and analyze pollution levels in nearby water sources. Through this hands-on approach, students apply theoretical knowledge and contribute positively to their communities, making learning both meaningful and impactful.

Another way to connect curriculum to real life is by incorporating interdisciplinary themes into the learning process. By linking subjects like mathematics, history, and art around a central topic—such as sustainability— students can explore complex issues from multiple perspectives. For instance, students might analyze historical data on climate change trends, use mathematical models to predict future impacts, and create artistic representations of these findings. This approach encourages critical thinking, deepens understanding, and provides a holistic view of the topic.

Inviting guest speakers from various professions into the classroom is another valuable way to demonstrate the relevance of academic concepts. For example, a mathematician could discuss the use of statistical analysis in sports, or an engineer might explain how design principles are applied in architecture. These real-world insights provide students with concrete examples of how their studies translate into practical applications, helping them envision how their education connects to potential career paths.

Connecting curriculum to real life, which is contextual learning in its simplest form, can also be achieved through community-based projects. By addressing real challenges within their local communities, students can see the direct impact of their learning. For instance, a civics class might work on drafting local policy proposals, or a business class might collaborate with small businesses to develop marketing strategies. These projects make learning relevant and instill a sense of purpose and responsibility within students.

Ultimately, connecting curriculum to real life empowers students by giving their education purpose and relevance. It encourages them to take ownership of their learning journey, develop practical skills, and build confidence in their ability to contribute meaningfully to society. By embracing strategies that link academic content to real-world applications, educators can help students see the value of their education and prepare them to navigate the complexities of modern life successfully.

The use of technology has further expanded the possibilities for contextual learning. Tools such as virtual reality (VR) and augmented reality (AR) offer immersive experiences that replicate real-world scenarios tied to the curriculum. For example, a history class might use VR to transport students to pivotal historical events or iconic locations, enabling them to explore the past in an interactive and engaging way. These technologies captivate students' attention while enhancing their comprehension of complex subjects by providing hands-on and visualized learning experiences.

Incorporating culturally relevant materials into lessons is another key aspect of contextual learning. By drawing on diverse perspectives and examples from different cultures, educators validate students' unique backgrounds and lived experiences. This practice promotes inclusivity and fosters a sense of belonging, as students see their identities reflected in the curriculum.

Engaging students through contextual learning transforms traditional educational practices into meaningful experiences that prepare them for real- world challenges. By linking academic content to practical applications and real-life contexts, educators empower students to take ownership of their learning and cultivate the critical thinking skills essential for success in a complex and ever-evolving society.

Building Interest and Curiosity

Building interest and curiosity in students is a cornerstone of effective education, as it lays the foundation for lifelong learning. When students are genuinely curious about a topic, they are more likely to engage deeply, retain information, and develop a meaningful understanding of the subject matter. To foster this intrinsic motivation, educators can employ various strategies that spark curiosity and inspire a love for learning.

One impactful method to help build curiosity and interest is inquiry-based learning, where students are encouraged to ask questions and explore topics that captivate their interest. By shifting the focus from passive information delivery to active exploration, educators create an environment where curiosity drives the learning process. Instead of presenting a lecture on ecosystems, a teacher might pose open-ended questions like, "What would happen if a keystone species disappeared?" Such questions prompt students to think critically and seek answers through research, experimentation, and collaborative discussion.

As noted in Chapter 2, storytelling is another powerful way to build interest and curiosity. Narratives engage students emotionally and make complex subjects more relatable by weaving information into memorable stories. History lessons can come alive when teachers share personal accounts of individuals who experienced significant events, allowing students to connect with historical figures on a human level. These stories captivate attention and foster empathy, making the material more engaging and meaningful.

Incorporating hands-on activities further enhances student interest by providing opportunities for experiential learning. Activities such as science experiments, art projects, and interactive simulations allow students to actively participate in their education rather than passively receiving information.

These practical experiences bridge gaps between theory and application, helping students internalize concepts through direct involvement and real- world problem-solving.

Equally important is fostering a classroom culture that celebrates curiosity. Educators should encourage students to ask questions, take risks, and view mistakes as opportunities for growth. Praising effort and exploration over correctness helps create a supportive environment where curiosity can thrive. Teachers can also model curiosity by sharing their own interests, discoveries, and enthusiasm for learning, inspiring students to adopt a similar mindset.

Cultivating interest and curiosity in students is essential for meaningful and lasting engagement with learning. By implementing inquiry-based approaches, storytelling, hands-on activities, and fostering a supportive classroom culture, educators can create an environment where curiosity flourishes. This has the power to enhance the educational experience and equip students with the tools and mindset to pursue lifelong learning with enthusiasm and confide

5

MINDFULNESS IN EDUCATION

Mindfulness has become a critical element in education, benefiting both teachers and students by fostering awareness, emotional regulation, and wellbeing. By integrating mindfulness into the classroom, educators can create a supportive and harmonious environment that enhances learning and personal growth. This section explores the importance of mindfulness for both teachers and students, highlighting its transformative effects on the educational experience.

For teachers, mindfulness offers a practical tool for managing the stress and demands of their profession. Educators often face challenges such as heavy workloads, classroom management issues, and the emotional labor of addressing students' diverse needs. Incorporating mindfulness practices like meditation, deep breathing, or reflective journaling can help teachers develop calmness, focus, and resilience. These practices reduce stress and enable teachers to engage with students more empathetically, creating a nurturing learning atmosphere.

Students also derive significant benefits from mindfulness practices. Research shows that engaging in mindfulness activities—such as breathing or guided imagery—helps reduce anxiety, improve concentration, and enhance emotional regulation. These effects are particularly valuable during stressful situations, such as exams or public speaking. By teaching students to be present and aware of their thoughts and emotions, educators equip them with skills that extend beyond academics, cultivating emotional intelligence and resilience in everyday life.

The impact of mindfulness can be observed in several key areas:

- **Enhanced focus**
  Mindfulness helps both teachers and students improve concentration and stay present with their tasks.

- **Emotional regulation**
  Regular mindfulness practice supports effective management of emotions.

- **Stress reduction**
  Mindfulness techniques reduce stress levels for all participants, contributing to a calmer classroom environment.

Beyond individual benefits, mindfulness also plays an important role in shaping a positive school culture. A mindful approach promotes empathy, respect, and collaboration among students and staff, creating an environment where everyone feels valued and supported. As schools increasingly integrate social-emotional learning alongside academic instruction, mindfulness becomes an essential evidenced-based strategy for nurturing well-rounded individuals capable of navigating life's challenges with confidence and self-awareness.

Breathing Techniques for Stress Management

Breathing techniques are an effective and accessible tool for managing stress, particularly in educational settings where both teachers and students often encounter high-pressure situations. These practices promote relaxation, enhance focus, and improve emotional regulation, making them an essential component of fostering a mindful and supportive learning environment.

One of the most effective techniques is **diaphragmatic breathing**, which involves engaging the diaphragm fully while inhaling deeply through the nose and exhaling slowly through the mouth. This method activates the body's relaxation response by reducing heart rate and lowering blood pressure. For educators, taking just a few minutes to practice diaphragmatic breathing before entering the classroom can help them approach their teaching with greater clarity, patience, and calmness. The practice also serves as a reset tool during challenging moments in the school day.

DIAPHRAGMATIC BREATHING

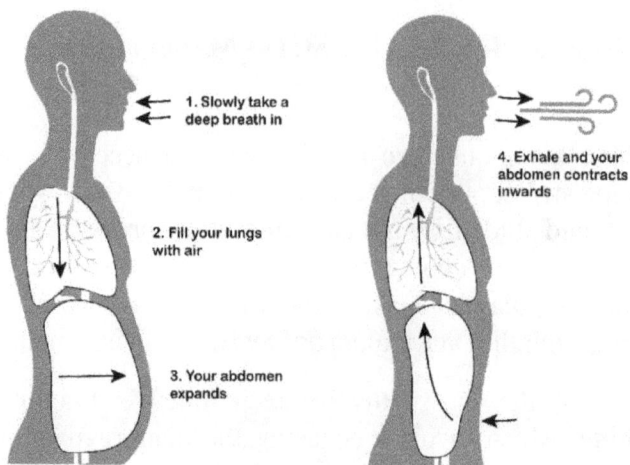

1. Slowly take a deep breath in

2. Fill your lungs with air

3. Your abdomen expands

4. Exhale and your abdomen contracts inwards

One simple, yet powerful breathing exercise is the **4-7-8 breathing method**: inhale for four counts, hold for seven counts, and exhale for eight counts. This rhythmic pattern calms racing thoughts and redirects attention to the present moment, helping students regain focus and reduce physiological signs of stress.

Schools that integrate mindfulness programs and dedicate time for guided breathing exercises often report improved behavior, enhanced academic performance, and reduced teacher burnout. Breathing techniques are more than just stress management tools—they are lifelong skills that prepare individuals to navigate challenges with composure, calmness and confidence.

Gratitude Practices in the Classroom

Gratitude practices in the classroom can be a powerful tool to use for fostering a positive learning environment. By embedding gratitude into daily routines, schools can cultivate resilience, strengthen relationships, and create a sense of community. These practices contribute to a more harmonious and supportive classroom dynamic while nurturing individual emotional growth.

One effective method of implementing this practice is starting a **gratitude circle** at the beginning or end of the school day. In this practice, students take turns sharing something they are grateful for, whether related to their personal lives or classroom experiences. This simple activity not only encourages self- reflection but also fosters empathy as students listen to one another's expressions of appreciation. Gratitude circles help build deeper connections among peers and establish an atmosphere where kindness and appreciation are valued.

Another impactful approach is the use of gratitude journals. By dedicating a few minutes each day to writing down three things they are thankful for, students practice mindfulness and shift their focus away from stress or negativity.

Research has shown that regular gratitude journaling can increase happiness and reduce symptoms of depression, particularly among adolescents. Teachers can guide this activity by offering prompts or themes related to the curriculum, such as "What is something new you learned today that you're grateful for?"

Art projects can also be an engaging way to integrate gratitude into the classroom. Allowing students to express their feelings creatively reinforces positive emotions and strengthens their emotional connections to others.

Additionally, celebrating **"Thank You" days**—where students write letters or create cards to express appreciation for teachers, staff, or classmates—fosters a sense of gratitude and community spirit.

These practices benefit individual students and also contribute to a positive classroom environment. Educators who model gratitude —by acknowledging student efforts and expressing appreciation—reinforce these values and set the tone for a supportive learning space. Ultimately, incorporating gratitude into educational practices creates an enduring culture of appreciation that extends beyond the classroom, preparing students for emotionally intelligent and compassionate interactions throughout their lives.

6

CREATING AN INCLUSIVE CLASSROOM ENVIRONMENT

Recognizing and embracing the diversity of learning styles is essential for creating an inclusive and equitable classroom environment. Each student comes with a unique set of experiences, preferences, and cognitive processes that shape how they absorb, process, and retain information. By understanding these differences, educators can adapt their teaching strategies to better meet the needs of all students and ensure that every learner can succeed.

Learning styles are often categorized into visual, auditory, kinesthetic, and reading/writing preferences. Visual learners benefit from tools such as diagrams, charts, and videos, while auditory learners excel through discussions, lectures, and verbal explanations. Kinesthetic learners engage best through hands-on activities, and reading/writing learners prefer working with written texts and taking notes. However, it is important to note that most students do not fit neatly into a single category; instead, they often exhibit a blend of these styles. Recognizing this overlap allows educators to approach teaching with greater flexibility.

Cultural background also plays a significant role in influencing learning preferences. For example, students from collectivist cultures may thrive in collaborative tasks that emphasize group harmony and shared success, while those from individualistic cultures might prefer independent projects that allow for personal expression and autonomy. By understanding and honoring these cultural nuances, educators can design lessons that resonate with diverse student populations, fostering an inclusive learning environment.

Incorporating varied teaching methods helps address the diversity of learning styles and enhances overall classroom engagement. For instance, project-based learning allows students to explore concepts using multiple modalities. A single project might include research (catering to reading/writing learners), presentations (supporting auditory learners), and practical applications (engaging kinesthetic learners). This integrative approach accommodates a range of preferences and promotes critical thinking, creativity, and problem- solving skills.

Ultimately, understanding and addressing diversity in learning styles is about recognizing the individuality of each learner and adapting instructional practices accordingly. This approach improves academic outcomes and also cultivates a sense of belonging and inclusion within the classroom community. By fostering an environment where all students feel seen and supported, educators can inspire confidence and a lifelong love of learning.

Strategies for Inclusivity & Accessibility

Creating an inclusive and accessible classroom environment is essential for fostering a sense of belonging among all students. Inclusivity involves implementing strategies that accommodate diverse learning needs, remove barriers, and encourage active participation. By prioritizing equity, educators can ensure that every student has meaningful access to learning opportunities and feels valued within the classroom community.

One effective strategy for promoting inclusivity is the adoption of **Universal Design for Learning (UDL)**. This approach emphasizes flexibility in teaching methods and materials, ensuring that lessons are accessible to a wide range of learners. UDL encourages educators to provide multiple means of representation, expression, and engagement. For example, offering content through diverse formats—such as videos, podcasts, text-based resources, and interactive simulations—allows students to choose the medium that aligns best with their preferences and needs. This strategy supports students with varied learning styles and also reduces barriers for those with disabilities by presenting information in ways that are adaptable and inclusive.

The physical layout of the classroom also plays a crucial role in accessibility. An accessible environment should be designed to accommodate all learners, including those with mobility challenges and sensory sensitivities. This might involve arranging furniture to allow easy movement, ensuring pathways are unobstructed, and providing adaptive tools such as height-adjustable desks and ergonomic seating. Additionally, the integration of assistive technologies, such as speech-to-text software, screen readers, and communication devices, can further enhance accessibility for students with specific needs. For students with sensory sensitivities, creating a quiet space with noise-reducing headphones and dimmable lighting can provide a calming environment that minimizes overstimulation.

Collaboration among peers is another key component of inclusivity. Structured group work promotes interaction across diverse perspectives and allows students to build on each other's strengths. Educators can support this by assigning roles within groups that align with individual skills while ensuring that each student contributes meaningfully to the task. This approach fosters teamwork and cultivates an appreciation for diversity within the classroom.

Training in cultural competency, implicit bias recognition, and inclusive practices equips educators with the tools to support all students effectively. These sessions can help teachers understand the importance of cultural differences, adapt to various learning needs, and build stronger connections with their students. Fostering a sense of belonging in the classroom is essential for student engagement, motivation, and academic success. When students feel valued as members of their learning community, they are more likely to participate actively, build meaningful relationships, and take academic risks.

Creating opportunities for personal connections among students is a highly effective way to foster a sense of belonging in the classroom. Icebreaker activities at the beginning of the school year or semester allow students to share their interests, backgrounds, and experiences. These activities help break down social barriers and encourage empathy and understanding. For example, pairing students for collaborative projects based on shared interests can enhance teamwork skills and promote the development of deeper interpersonal relationships.

Incorporating culturally responsive teaching practices is another powerful approach to promoting belonging. By integrating diverse perspectives into the curriculum—such as literature from different cultures or historical events reflecting multiple viewpoints, educators validate students' identities and experiences. This representation helps students see themselves within the content being taught, reinforcing their sense of belonging and inclusion in the classroom.

Clear and consistent communication between educators and students also plays a critical role in creating a sense of belonging. Regular check-ins, through surveys or informal conversations, provide valuable insights into how students perceive their role in the classroom community. Establishing an open-door policy encourages students to share concerns, ask questions, or seek support without fear of judgment, fostering trust and rapport.

- **Encouraging peer mentorship program**
  Older or more experienced students supporting newcomers can enhance feelings of inclusion.

- **Celebrating cultural diversity**
  Themed days and events allow students to showcase their heritage while promoting mutual respect.

- **Implementing restorative practices**
  Addressing conflicts through dialogue and reconciliation fosters a supportive environment focused on healing and growth rather than punishment.

Ultimately, it requires a continuous commitment from educators to create inclusive spaces where every student feels respected, supported, and valued. By implementing these strategies, teachers can cultivate a vibrant classroom culture that empowers all learners to thrive both academically, physically and socially.

7

GROWTH MINDSET
PRINCIPLES

The concept of a growth mindset, popularized by psychologist Carol Dweck, is a transformative framework in education that reshapes how students view their abilities and potential. A growth mindset emphasizes that intelligence and skills can be developed through effort, perseverance, and learning from failures. This perspective contrasts with a fixed mindset, where abilities are perceived as static and unchangeable. Fostering a growth mindset in education is essential for cultivating resilient learners who embrace challenges and view setbacks as opportunities for growth.

Implementing a growth mindset in the classroom involves several foundational principles. First, educators must model this mindset by exhibiting a passion for learning and openly discussing their own challenges and failures. Sharing personal stories about overcoming obstacles or acquiring new skills normalizes the struggles inherent in the learning process and demonstrates that growth is achievable for everyone.

Classroom practices should also prioritize effort and strategy over innate ability. Feedback plays a critical role in this shift, as it encourages students to focus on the process rather than the outcome. For instance, praising students for their perseverance and the strategies they employ to solve problems reinforces the value of persistence and adaptability. Collaborative learning experiences further strengthen this perspective by allowing students to learn from each other's approaches, highlighting that growth is a shared and dynamic process.

Reflection is another vital component of fostering a growth mindset. Encouraging students to evaluate their own learning journeys helps them recognize progress and appreciate that mastery is a gradual process requiring consistent effort. Reflective practices such as journaling, goal-setting, or peer discussions about challenges faced during projects provide opportunities for students to analyze their development and build confidence in their abilities to improve.

Defining and fostering a growth mindset in education extends beyond terminology; it requires systemic changes in teaching philosophy and daily practice. By embedding these principles into their interactions with students, educators improve academic outcomes and prepare learners with the mindset and skills necessary to navigate the complexities of an ever changing world.

Encouraging resilience and persistence is fundamental to fostering a growth mindset in educational settings. Resilience refers to the ability to recover from setbacks, while persistence is the determination to continue striving toward goals despite obstacles. Together, these qualities empower students to overcome challenges and transform failures into valuable learning opportunities.

An effective way to promote resilience is by highlighting real-life examples of perseverance. Educators can introduce accounts of individuals, whether historical figures, community leaders, or even personal experiences- who have faced adversity and overcome challenges to achieve their goals. For instance, recounting the experiences of figures like Thomas Edison or J.K. Rowling demonstrates that failure is often a stepping stone to success. These stories not only serve as sources of inspiration but also reinforce the idea that struggle and setbacks are integral parts of growth and achievement.

Creating a classroom environment that normalizes mistakes is equally important in fostering resilience. When educators emphasize that mistakes are opportunities for learning rather than indicators of failure, students feel more comfortable taking risks and engaging deeply in the learning process. Practices such as "error analysis," where students collaboratively examine and learn from their mistakes, can cultivate a culture of exploration and innovation without fear of judgment.

Setting incremental goals is another powerful strategy for encouraging persistence. Breaking larger tasks into smaller, achievable objectives allows students to experience regular success along their journey. These smaller victories build confidence and reinforce the understanding that progress often requires consistent effort over time. For example, a student working on a long- term project might set weekly milestones to stay motivated and focused.

Teaching self-regulation strategies further supports both resilience and persistence by equipping students with tools to manage their emotions and behaviors during challenging situations. Techniques such as mindfulness exercises, reflective journaling, and structured goal-setting frameworks enable learners to evaluate their progress, adjust their approaches, and stay motivated. These skills enhance academic performance and prepares students to navigate life's broader uncertainties with confidence and composure.

Fostering resilience and persistence in the classroom requires intentional strategies that inspire, support, and empower students to face challenges with determination. By sharing inspiring stories, normalizing mistakes, setting manageable goals, and teaching self-regulation, educators create an environment where students can grow through adversity and persist in achieving their goals.

Overcoming challenges with a growth perspective is fundamental to both personal and academic development. This approach encourages individuals to see obstacles not as barriers but as opportunities for growth and learning. By adopting this mindset, learners can cultivate resilience, enhance their problem-solving abilities, and deepen their understanding of their potential.

A critical element of overcoming challenges is reframing negative experiences. When difficulties arise, it is natural to feel frustration or defeat. However, consciously shifting focus to the lessons these situations provide can transform setbacks into opportunities for growth. For example, a student struggling in a particular subject might initially feel discouraged. By analyzing the root causes of their difficulties—whether it be ineffective study methods, gaps in understanding, or lack of focus—they can seek appropriate help and adopt new strategies that lead to improvement. This reframing builds problem-solving skills and reinforces the belief that challenges are surmountable.

Embracing failure as part of the learning process is another cornerstone of a growth perspective. Many successful individuals have openly shared stories of their failures before achieving their goals, such as athletes missing critical plays or entrepreneurs experiencing early setbacks in their ventures. These narratives highlight that failure is not an endpoint but a stepping stone to future success. Educators can integrate these examples into lessons to normalize failure, helping students understand that taking risks and making mistakes is essential for growth.

Also crucial in helping students overcome challenges with a growth mindset is to foster a highly supportive community. When learners are surrounded by peers and mentors who encourage exploration, experimentation, and perseverance, they are more likely to take risks and view challenges as opportunities. Collaborative activities, such as group projects and open discussions, provide a platform for students to share their experiences and strategies, reinforcing the idea that they are not alone in their struggles. This sense of shared effort builds confidence and solidarity.

Setting realistic expectations is equally important when approaching challenges. Progress is often incremental, and learners should recognize that growth requires consistent effort over time. Celebrating small victories—such as mastering a specific concept or improving on a previous attempt—reinforces persistence and boosts motivation. Acknowledging each step forward, no matter how small, builds confidence and prepares individuals to tackle larger obstacles in the future.

Overcoming challenges with a growth perspective requires intentional strategies that emphasize resilience, learning from failure, collaboration, and persistence. By reframing difficulties, embracing the learning process, facilitating supportive communities, and celebrating progress, learners are empowered to navigate challenges effectively and grow in both their abilities and confidence.

8

EMOTIONAL INTELLIGENCE IN THE CLASSROOM

Imagine a classroom where every learner feels genuinely supported and engaged—even on the toughest days. This vision is achievable through Emotional Intelligence (EI), which is the capacity to recognize, understand, and respond effectively to emotions. EI is crucial in education because it fosters respectful communication, reduces conflict, and motivates students to collaborate. Its three core components are recognizing emotions (in ourselves and others), cultivating empathy (to build deeper connections), and practicing emotional regulation (managing stress in constructive ways). This chapter explores how integrating these EI skills transforms a classroom into an inclusive, empathetic, and academically driven environment.

Recognizing Emotions - In Self & Others

Recognizing emotions in oneself and others is a cornerstone of emotional intelligence, particularly in educational settings. This skill enhances interpersonal relationships and creates a supportive learning environment where students feel understood and valued. By cultivating the ability to identify emotions, educators can better address students' needs, fostering an atmosphere that promotes both academic success and personal growth.

The process of recognizing emotions begins with self-awareness. Educators must first understand their own emotional states, as these can significantly impact their teaching effectiveness. For example, a teacher who recognizes signs of stress can employ strategies like mindfulness or breathing exercises to maintain composure during challenging situations. By demonstrating emotional self-regulation, educators model the importance of managing emotions, setting a positive example for students.

Recognizing emotions in others requires keen observation and active listening. Educators should pay attention to verbal cues, such as tone of voice, as well as non-verbal signals like body language and facial expressions. For instance, a student who appears withdrawn or avoids participation may be experiencing anxiety or frustration. Acknowledging these signs and initiating a supportive conversation can help validate students' feelings and provide guidance or reassurance.

Conducting regular check-ins with students

Allows educators to assess students' emotional well-being and address concerns early.

Creating safe spaces for expression

Encourages open communication and trust among peers, fostering a supportive classroom community.

Using role-playing exercises

Helps students recognize and navigate emotions in different scenarios, strengthening empathy and interpersonal skills.

Integrating social-emotional learning (SEL) into the curriculum further supports emotional recognition and articulation. Activities such as group discussions about emotional experiences, and lessons on empathy provide students with tools to navigate their emotions effectively and understand those of others. These practices nurture an emotionally intelligent classroom culture where students feel supported and connected. Prioritizing the recognition of emotions in oneself and others is essential for building an empathetic and resilient classroom community. By modeling self-awareness, observing and responding to students' emotional cues, and incorporating SEL practices, educators lay the foundation for a learning environment that values emotional intelligence, collaboration, and holistic growth.

Developing Empathy

Empathy is a fundamental element of emotional intelligence that greatly enhances the classroom environment. By fostering empathy, educators can cultivate a culture of understanding and respect, improving interpersonal relationships, encouraging academic collaboration, and promoting emotional well-being. Developing empathy enables students to connect with their peers on a deeper level, creating an inclusive atmosphere where everyone feels valued and heard.

One effective way to nurture empathy is through structured group activities that emphasize perspective-taking. For example, literature discussions can challenge students to imagine themselves in the shoes of characters from diverse backgrounds or experiences. This exercise broadens their understanding of different viewpoints and fosters an appreciation for the complexities of human emotions and motivations.

Similarly, incorporating service-learning projects into the curriculum provides students with real-world opportunities to engage with communities outside their own, strengthening their empathetic skills and understanding of social issues.

Role-playing exercises also serve as powerful tools for fostering empathy in the classroom. Simulating scenarios such as conflict resolution or providing peer support allows students to practice responding to others' feelings in a safe and guided environment. These activities encourage active listening, thoughtful responses, and the consideration of others' perspectives. Reflective discussions following these exercises deepen students' understanding of emotions and their impact on interactions, reinforcing the value of empathy in daily life.

Some additional ideas to assist students practice empathy are as follows,

- **Encouraging reflective journaling:**
  This provides students with an outlet to express their thoughts and feelings while contemplating how their actions affect others.

- **Creating a "kindness wall":**
  Showcases acts of kindness, fostering a culture of empathy and appreciation within the classroom .

- ## Integrating multimedia resources:
  Using films and documentaries to spark discussions on social issues, deepening students' understanding of empathy and its broader impact.

Developing empathy among students is essential for creating a harmonious learning environment that prioritizes emotional connections. By implementing diverse strategies such as group activities, role-playing, reflective practices, and multimedia engagement, educators empower students to grow into socially responsible individuals. This focus not only enhances academic success but also equips students with the compassion and understanding necessary to make positive contributions to the broader community.

Tools for Emotional Regulation

Emotional regulation is a critical skill that helps students manage their emotions effectively, creating a supportive and productive learning environment. Empowering students with strategies to navigate their feelings, educators can foster improved academic performance, better interpersonal relationships, and greater emotional resilience. This section explores various techniques that can be implemented in the classroom to enhance students' ability to regulate their emotions.

One highly effective tool for emotional regulation is mindfulness practice. Mindfulness encourages students to focus on the present moment, allowing them to become more aware of their thoughts and feelings without judgment. Simple breathing exercises, such as the techniques discussed in Chapter 5, and guided meditation sessions can be seamlessly integrated into daily routines. For example, beginning each class with a brief mindfulness activity helps students center themselves, fostering a calm and focused mindset conducive to learning.

Regular Emotion check-ins provide students with a structured way to express their feelings, helping educators foster a supportive and emotionally aware classroom environment. By creating a safe space where students can express their feelings, educators normalize emotional discussions and promote self-awareness. Simple tools like color-coded cards or mood meters displayed in the classroom allow students to communicate their emotions easily. For instance, students might select a color that represents their mood at the start of the day, giving teachers insight into their emotional state and enabling timely support when needed.

Journaling is also an excellent tool for emotional regulation. Encouraging students to write about their daily experiences and emotions provides them with a constructive outlet for processing feelings.

Educators can offer prompts that guide students in reflecting on specific situations, helping them recognize patterns in their emotional responses and develop effective coping strategies over time.

Outlined below are several additional tools for practicing emotional regulation.

- **Engaging in role-play scenarios**
  Providing students with opportunities to navigate challenging emotional situations in a safe, controlled environment builds confidence and strengthens their ability to manage real-life interactions.

- **Incorporating visual emotion charts**
  Helping younger learners identify and label their feelings accurately supports early emotional literacy and fosters self-

awareness.

- **Establishing peer support systems**
  Encouraging students to assist one another during emotional challenges promotes collaboration and strengthens classroom relationships.

Providing students with tools for emotional regulation not only enhances their ability to manage their emotions but also improves overall classroom dynamics by promoting empathy and mutual understanding. By integrating these strategies into everyday teaching practices, educators play a vital role in nurturing emotionally intelligent individuals.

9

COLLABORATIVE LEARNING STRATEGIES

The ability to work effectively in teams is essential for both academic achievement and future workplace readiness. Collaborative learning leverages peer interaction to deepen understanding, enhance critical thinking, and cultivate social skills such as empathy and conflict resolution. By engaging in well-structured group activities, students build stronger content mastery and develop the adaptability and communication abilities needed beyond the classroom. This chapter examines the importance of peer collaboration, outlines strategies for effectively structuring group work, and discusses comprehensive approaches to assessing collaborative efforts in a supportive, interactive learning environment.

Peer interaction is a foundational element of collaborative learning, significantly enriching the educational experience for students. Engaging with peers creates a dynamic environment where learners exchange diverse perspectives, challenge one another's ideas, and collaboratively construct knowledge. This process deepens understanding while fostering essential social skills that are invaluable both academically and in real-world contexts.

A primary benefit of peer interaction is the enhancement of critical thinking skills. When students engage in group discussions or collaborative projects, they are required to articulate their thoughts clearly, evaluate opposing viewpoints, and justify their reasoning. These activities encourage analytical thinking and expose students to alternative perspectives, leading to more comprehensive cognitive development. For instance, students involved in peer- led discussions often demonstrate improved performance on tasks requiring higher-order thinking compared to those who learn in isolation.

Peer interaction also plays a crucial role in boosting motivation and engagement. Collaborative tasks create a sense of accountability and interdependence within groups. When students recognize that their contributions affect the group's overall success, they are more likely to invest effort into their work. This collective responsibility fosters a supportive learning environment where students feel motivated to participate actively. For example, project-based learning initiatives frequently observe increased student enthusiasm and involvement when peers collaborate closely.

In addition to academic benefits, peer interactions significantly contribute to emotional and social development. Working with others helps students develop empathy by exposing them to diverse opinions and experiences. It also provides opportunities to practice essential interpersonal skills, such as conflict resolution and negotiation. By engaging with peers from different cultural or socio-economic backgrounds, students gain broader insights into global perspectives and develop a deeper appreciation for diversity.

Structuring Group Activities

Effective structuring of group activities is essential for maximizing the benefits of collaborative learning. When designed thoughtfully, these activities enhance student engagement, deepen understanding, and develop key skills such as teamwork, communication, and problem-solving. The structure of a group activity significantly influences its outcomes, making it critical for educators to carefully plan and implement strategies that promote successful collaboration.

A foundational element of structuring group activities is defining clear objectives. Educators must articulate specific goals that align with the desired learning outcomes. For example, if the aim is to strengthen critical thinking skills, the activity might involve analyzing a multifaceted problem where students collaboratively evaluate various solutions. Clearly defined objectives ensure that students understand the purpose of their collaboration and remain focused and engaged throughout the process.

Group composition is another crucial consideration. Diverse groups that include a mix of skill levels, backgrounds, and perspectives enrich discussions and foster innovative thinking. Educators can use strategies like heterogeneous grouping (combining students of different abilities, backgrounds or learning styles) or random assignment to ensure diversity within teams. Assigning specific roles within groups—such as facilitator, note-taker, or presenter— helps clarify responsibilities and ensures active participation from all members. These roles also encourage accountability and equitable contributions within the group.

Time management is equally important in structuring effective group activities. Providing sufficient time for discussion and collaboration while setting clear deadlines helps maintain productivity and focus. Incorporating periodic checkpoints during the activity allows groups to assess their progress, receive guidance, and make adjustments as needed. These structured intervals ensure that students stay on track without feeling rushed or overwhelmed.

Feedback mechanisms further enhance the effectiveness of group activities by encouraging reflection and continuous improvement. Peer evaluations, self- assessments, or guided group discussions following the activity allow students to evaluate their performance and identify areas for growth. Reflecting on both individual and group contributions fosters a deeper understanding of collaborative dynamics and prepares students for future teamwork.

Assessing collaborative work is an essential aspect of effective educational practice, as it evaluates the outcomes of group activities, the dynamics and contributions of individual members. A well-structured assessment process provides valuable insights into how students work together to achieve shared goals while identifying areas for improvement in both academic and interpersonal skills.

A key element of assessing collaborative work is establishing clear criteria that address both individual and group performance. These criteria should encompass dimensions such as participation, communication, problem-solving abilities, and the quality of the final product. For example, educators can use rubrics to outline specific expectations for each role within the group, ensuring accountability and fairness. Clear and transparent criteria provide students with a framework to understand what is expected of them and encourage a sense of responsibility for their contributions.

Incorporating self-assessment and peer evaluation into the assessment process can further enhance its effectiveness. Structured tools, such as feedback forms or guided reflection sessions, enable students to evaluate their own contributions as well as those of their peers. This practice encourages self-awareness, metacognition, and also fosters critical skills in giving and receiving constructive feedback. Students learn to reflect on their strengths and areas for growth, which can improve their performance in future collaborations.

Ongoing formative assessments during the collaborative process are also invaluable. Regular check-ins or progress reports provide educators with real- time insights into group dynamics and individual engagement levels. These informal assessments allow instructors to address potential challenges—such as uneven participation or communication breakdowns—early in the process, ensuring that groups remain productive and cohesive.

Finally, assessing collaborative work should extend beyond academic performance to include interpersonal skills such as conflict resolution, empathy, adaptability, and teamwork. Recognizing and valuing these soft skills alongside academic outcomes prepares students for real-world scenarios where collaboration is critical. Highlighting these competencies in assessment criteria reinforces their importance and encourages students to cultivate them intentionally.

To recap, effective assessment of collaborative work involves a combination of clear criteria, self and peer evaluations, formative assessments, and recognition of interpersonal skills. By implementing a holistic approach to assessing group activities, educators can ensure that students achieve academic success and develop the critical collaborative abilities needed for lifelong learning and professional success.

10

TECHNOLOGY INTEGRATION IN TEACHING

The integration of educational technology is important in enhancing student engagement and optimizing learning outcomes. By leveraging technology effectively, educators can create dynamic and inclusive classrooms that address diverse learning needs and preferences. This section explores strategies for utilizing educational technology to foster a more interactive, personalized, and impactful learning environment.

One of the primary advantages of educational technology is its ability to facilitate differentiated instruction. Adaptive learning platforms tailor content to meet individual student needs, enabling learners to progress at their own pace. Tools like Khan Academy provide personalized practice exercises that adjust based on a student's performance, ensuring that each learner encounters the appropriate level of challenge and support. This customization helps bridge gaps in understanding while advancing stronger students toward more complex material. Incorporating multimedia resources into lessons also enhances understanding and retention by catering to various learning styles. Visual aids, videos, and interactive simulations make complex concepts more accessible and engaging. For example, platforms like Nearpod allow teachers to design immersive lessons that integrate video content, real-time assessments, and interactive activities, encouraging active participation and deeper comprehension among students.

Collaboration tools are another essential component of educational technology, fostering communication and teamwork in modern classrooms. Platforms such as Google Classroom streamline resource sharing, peer feedback, and instructor-student communication, promoting collaboration on projects and assignments. These tools enhance social skills and prepare students for future professional environments where teamwork and digital literacy are vital.

Additionally, educational technology provides opportunities for data-driven instruction. Learning management systems (LMS) and other digital assessment tools generate performance metrics that enable educators to monitor student progress and identify areas of difficulty. By analyzing this data, teachers can adapt their instructional strategies to address specific challenges, ensuring that interventions are timely and effective. This personalized approach supports improved outcomes for all learners.

Utilizing educational technology extends beyond the integration of tools; it requires reimagining teaching practices to create more engaging, inclusive, and effective learning experiences. By thoughtfully adopting and implementing these technologies, educators can unlock new pathways for student growth, foster collaboration, and ensure that all learners reach their full potential.

Enhancing Engagement

In today's educational landscape, enhancing student engagement is a critical component of effective teaching. Digital tools provide innovative solutions to capture students' attention and foster active participation, transforming traditional learning into a more dynamic and interactive experience. By integrating these technologies into their practices, educators can create environments that inspire motivation, collaboration, and critical thinking.

One of the most impactful ways to boost engagement is through gamification. Incorporating game-like elements such as points, badges, and leaderboards transforms routine tasks into exciting challenges. Platforms like Kahoot!, allow educators to design interactive quizzes that promote friendly competition and active participation. This approach makes learning enjoyable while reinforcing knowledge retention through repeated practice in a fun, engaging format.

Immersive technologies (like VR and AR mentioned in chapter 4) are also revolutionizing how students engage with content. These tools provide hands- on experiences that bring abstract concepts to life. For instance, VR headsets can take students on virtual field trips to historical landmarks or enable them to conduct complex science experiments in a simulated environment. These experiences deepen understanding, spark curiosity, and make learning memorable by allowing students to visualize and interact with material in unique ways.

Social media platforms offer additional opportunities for enhancing engagement. Educators can use tools like Twitter, Instagram, or dedicated class apps to encourage collaboration and showcase student work. Creating class accounts where learners share projects, ideas, or reflections fosters a sense of community and extends learning beyond the classroom. These platforms also prepare students for real-world communication skills that are increasingly important in the digital age.

Digital storytelling tools further enrich engagement by enabling students to express creativity while mastering academic content. Applications like Microsoft PowerPoint and Adobe Spark empower students to create multimedia presentations that integrate text, images, and videos, allowing them to take ownership of their learning process. This hands-on approach enhances understanding and encourages active participation.

In today's evolving educational landscape, striking a balance between screen time and traditional teaching methods is essential for fostering a well-rounded learning experience. As digital tools play an increasingly prominent role in classrooms, educators must ensure that technology enhances student engagement and understanding without overshadowing the benefits of conventional approaches.

One critical consideration in achieving this balance is addressing the cognitive impact of excessive screen time. Research shows that prolonged screen exposure can lead to reduced attention spans and hinder information retention. To mitigate these effects, educators can establish structured guidelines for screen usage. For example, incorporating designated "screen-free" periods during lessons allows students to participate in hands-on activities such as group discussions, problem-solving exercises, or creative projects. These activities promote collaboration, critical thinking, and deeper engagement with the material.

Blending traditional methods with technology creates a more dynamic and inclusive learning environment. For example, educators might use digital tools for research, interactive simulations, or presentations while incorporating conventional methods like reading physical books, writing by hand, or engaging in classroom debates. This combination diversifies learning experiences, catering to different preferences and styles while ensuring that students develop a broad range of skills. Alternating between digital and traditional resources helps maintain interest and reinforces understanding by presenting content in multiple formats.

Integrating physical and experiential activities further counterbalances sedentary screen time. Lessons that involve role-playing, outdoor science experiments, or art projects provide students with opportunities to apply their knowledge in real-world contexts. These active, hands-on approaches enhance comprehension while also addressing the physical and emotional benefits of movement and interaction.

Achieving a balance between screen time and traditional methods requires ongoing reflection and adaptability from educators. Regularly assessing the effectiveness of both approaches ensures that instructional strategies remain relevant, engaging, and impactful. By leveraging technology to complement rather than replace traditional teaching, educators can cultivate learners who are digitally proficient and equipped with the critical thinking and interpersonal skills necessary for success.

11

Assessment Techniques Aligned with Neuroscience

Assessing student progress is more than just assigning final scores - it is a deliberate process that shapes instruction, nurtures growth, and reinforces learning pathways in the brain. By aligning assessment strategies with neuroscience principles, educators can move beyond rote memorization and create meaningful evaluations that deepen comprehension. This chapter examines how formative and summative assessments, timely feedback, and well-designed tasks can collectively drive engagement and mastery, ensuring that each learner's true understanding is both cultivated and recognized.

Formative vs. Summative Assessments

Understanding the distinction between formative and summative assessments is essential for educators aiming to optimize learning outcomes through neuroscience-informed practices. Each type of assessment serves a unique purpose, shaping how students engage with material and guiding educators in tailoring their instructional strategies.

Formative assessments are ongoing evaluations conducted during the learning process. They provide immediate feedback to both students and teachers, enabling timely adjustments to instruction based on student needs. Techniques such as quizzes, peer reviews, and classroom discussions exemplify formative assessments. Neuroscience underscores the value of these frequent check-ins, as they reinforce neural pathways associated with learning and memory retention. timely feedback helps students correct misunderstandings before they become ingrained, fostering a growth mindset and building confidence in their abilities.

In contrast, summative assessments measure student learning at the end of an instructional unit by evaluating their performance against a specific standard or benchmark. Examples include final exams, standardized tests, and end-of- term projects. Summative assessments are critical for assessing overall achievement and ensuring accountability. However, they often lack the immediacy of formative assessments. Neuroscientific research reveals that high-stakes testing can trigger stress responses in students, potentially compromising performance by causing anxiety rather than accurately measuring their true knowledge or abilities.

The interplay between formative and summative assessments is key to developing a balanced and effective assessment strategy. Formative assessments provide actionable insights that inform and improve teaching practices in real time, while summative assessments offer a broader perspective on students' long-term retention and understanding.

Together, these approaches support differentiated instruction by addressing individual learning needs and promoting equitable opportunities for success.

Integrating both assessment types aligns with principles of neuroeducation by recognizing the diverse trajectories of learning. A thoughtful combination of formative and summative assessments helps educators create an inclusive environment where all students feel supported and motivated. By incorporating insights from neuroscience regarding memory retention, feedback, and stress management, teachers can design assessment strategies that measure achievement, enhance engagement, and deepen understanding.

Feedback Mechanisms

Feedback mechanisms are important tools in education, particularly when designed with neuroscience principles in mind. They serve not only to inform students about their performance but also to encourage a growth mindset, fostering resilience and continuous improvement. Understanding how to implement effective feedback is essential for educators seeking to enhance student engagement and achievement.

One of the most impactful feedback strategies is providing **timely and specific feedback**. Neuroscience research highlights that immediate responses to student work can significantly enhance learning by reinforcing neural pathways associated with the material. The degree of impact can depend on factors such as the complexity of the task, the learner's cognitive load, and how the feedback is delivered.

For example, when teachers provide constructive comments shortly after an assignment is submitted, students are more likely to retain the information and apply it in future tasks.

Prompt feedback helps prevent misconceptions from becoming ingrained, allowing learners to adjust their understanding dynamically.

Equally important is framing feedback in a **positive and constructive manner**. Highlighting strengths alongside areas for improvement creates a supportive environment where students feel valued and capable of growth. This approach aligns with Carol Dweck's concept of a growth mindset, which emphasizes that individuals who view abilities as malleable through effort are more likely to embrace challenges and persist in the face of setbacks.

Additional formats of feedback which benefit students are as follows

- **Peer Feedback**
  Encouraging students to provide feedback to their peers fosters collaboration, critical thinking, and exposure to diverse perspectives. It also enables students to reflect on their own understanding as they evaluate others' work.

- **Self-Assessment**
  Teaching students how to evaluate their own work cultivates metacognitive skills, helping them recognize their strengths and independently identify areas for improvement in.

- **Goal-Oriented Feedback**
  Providing specific, actionable goals helps students focus

on clear targets for improvement, making the feedback process more meaningful and manageable.

The integration of technology into feedback mechanisms offers additional opportunities to promote growth. Digital platforms enable real-time feedback through interactive assessments, online discussions, or even automated tools that highlight areas for improvement. These resources engage students in the learning process while catering to various learning styles, and allows teachers to deliver personalized comments efficiently, ensuring students receive timely and detailed responses.

feedback mechanisms designed with neuroscience principles not only inform students but also inspire them to grow. By prioritizing timely, positive, and goal-oriented feedback, alongside peer interactions, self-assessment, and the use of technology, educators can create a learning environment that supports continuous improvement.

Assessment Design

Designing assessments that truly reflect a student's understanding is fundamental for effective education, particularly when guided by neuroscience principles. Traditional assessment methods often emphasize rote memorization or standardized testing, which may fail to capture the depth of a student's comprehension. By aligning assessments with how the brain learns and processes information, educators can create meaningful evaluations that encourage genuine understanding.

One of the most effective ways to assess comprehension is through authentic assessments that require students to apply their knowledge in meaningful, real-world contexts. For younger students, this might involve designing and testing a bridge using everyday materials to explore engineering principles, creating a class newspaper to develop writing and research skills, or planning a community garden to understand ecosystems and sustainability. For older students, tasks such as designing a sustainable city model, developing a marketing campaign for a social cause, or crafting a legal argument for a mock trial encourages students to think critically, synthesize information, and make informed decisions. Neuroscience suggests that connecting new information to prior knowledge through experiential learning strengthens retention and deepens understanding. Additionally, assessments that incorporate structured reflection, debate, and collaborative problem-solving reinforce cognitive connections associated with higher-order thinking, ensuring students engage with content in a way that fosters long-term mastery.

Incorporating **diverse assessment formats** is equally important for addressing various learning styles and preferences. Alternative formats, such as visual presentations, group projects, or portfolios, provide students with multiple ways to demonstrate their understanding. These varied approaches keep students engaged and also offer educators a more comprehensive view of each learner's capabilities and progress.

Additionally, assessments should emphasize higher-order thinking skills rather than mere recall of facts. Tasks that require analysis, synthesis, and evaluation encourage students to go beyond surface-level understanding and engage deeply with the material. Open-ended questions, case studies, and design challenges are examples of assessment types that promote deeper cognitive engagement.

Designing assessments that reflect true understanding necessitates a shift from traditional testing to more dynamic and meaningful approaches grounded in neuroscience principles. By integrating formative assessments, authentic tasks, diverse formats, and higher-order thinking opportunities, educators can create an environment where comprehension flourishes and students are prepared to apply their knowledge in real-world scenarios and future learning endeavors.

12

BUILDING TEACHER-STUDENT RELATIONSHIPS

Building strong teacher-student relationships is fundamental to fostering a positive and effective learning environment. When students feel supported and valued, they are more engaged, motivated, and willing to take academic risks. Grounded in trust, communication, and inclusivity, these relationships enhance both cognitive and emotional development. This chapter explores the key strategies that educators can use to cultivate meaningful connections, create a supportive classroom atmosphere, and strengthen student confidence, ensuring that every learner feels empowered to succeed.

The Role of Trust in Learning

Trust is a foundational element in education, shaping the relationship between teachers and students - significantly impacting the learning process. A key way that trust enhances learning is by creating a sense of safety within the classroom. Students who trust their teachers are more likely to participate actively in discussions and share their thoughts without fear of judgment. This open communication enriches classroom interactions and promotes collaborative learning experiences.

When educators demonstrate genuine care for their students' well-being and academic growth, they create a positive emotional climate that enhances intrinsic motivation. Students are more likely to tackle challenging tasks when they believe their efforts will be recognized and valued. Recognition can take various forms, such as verbal praise, constructive feedback, or gestures of encouragement, reinforcing the idea that effort leads to growth. This sense of appreciation and acknowledgment strengthens students' confidence and perseverance.

Beyond individual relationships, trust contributes to building a cohesive classroom community. In environments where trust is nurtured, students develop empathy and mutual respect, fostering inclusivity and collaboration. A trusted classroom culture encourages students to support one another, to celebrate diverse perspectives, and engage collectively in learning, creating a strong foundation for holistic education.

Trust is the foundation of a thriving learning environment, shaping how students engage, take risks, and persevere. For younger students, storytelling circles—where teachers and students share personal experiences or reflections—help create emotional safety, fostering connection and open communication. For older students, collaborative goal-setting, where educators and students work together to define academic or personal growth targets, reinforces mutual respect and investment in the learning process.

By embedding trust-building practices into daily instruction, educators create a secure and supportive space where all students feel valued, confident, and ready to learn.

Communication Skills for Educators

Effective communication skills are crucial for successful teaching, shaping the foundation for strong teacher-student relationships and impactful learning experiences. The ability to convey information clearly and empathetically enhances student understanding and fosters a supportive, inclusive classroom environment. This section explores key dimensions of communication that educators must master to engage students meaningfully.

A critical component of effective communication is **active listening**. Educators who actively listen demonstrate respect for and validation of their students' thoughts and emotions. Active listening involves not only hearing the words students say but also interpreting the underlying feelings and intentions. For example, when a student expresses frustration over a challenging topic, an educator who listens attentively can empathize and provide tailored support or alternative explanations that align with the student's perspective. This approach builds trust and encourages open dialogue.

Non-verbal communication is another essential element of effective interaction in the classroom. Body language, facial expressions, and eye contact significantly influence how messages are perceived. An educator's enthusiasm, for instance, can be conveyed through animated gestures or an approachable posture, encouraging students to participate actively. Conversely, closed or disinterested body language may negatively impact engagement and create barriers to effective communication.

Equally important is **clarity in verbal communication**. Educators should strive to articulate ideas concisely and avoid jargon that could confuse students. Using relatable analogies, examples, or real-world applications can make complex concepts more accessible and engaging. Additionally, fostering an interactive learning environment by encouraging questions ensures that students feel comfortable seeking clarification and engaging with the material without fear of judgment.

Effective communication is indispensable for educators seeking to build strong connections with their students and facilitate meaningful learning. Active listening, clear expression, and thoughtful feedback help students feel valued, increasing their confidence, engagement, and overall academic growth.

Creating a Supportive Atmosphere

A classroom is more than a place for instruction—it's a space where students either feel safe to explore ideas or hesitate in fear of judgment. Neuroscience shows that emotional security directly impacts cognitive function, with trust and belonging enhancing focus, memory, and engagement. This section explores key strategies for cultivating an environment that promotes both academic and emotional growth.

Trust is foundational for creating a supportive atmosphere and positive learning space, as it directly influences the brain's limbic system, which regulates emotions and motivation. When students feel safe expressing their thoughts without fear of criticism, the brain reduces the release of stress- related cortisol, allowing for greater cognitive flexibility and engagement. Simple practices like daily peer-buddy check-ins for younger students, and anonymous feedback boxes for older students help educators assess well-being and provide timely support, reinforcing a culture of psychological safety and open communication.

Inclusivity further strengthens the learning environment by activating the brain's reward pathways, particularly through social belonging and recognition. Educators can promote inclusivity by incorporating diverse perspectives into lessons, facilitating discussions that encourage open dialogue, and structuring collaborative activities, such as group projects. These approaches help to build stronger social connections and create an atmosphere where all students feel engaged and valued.

The physical environment of the classroom also plays a key role in creating a supportive atmosphere. **Designing an inviting space**—adorned with student artwork, comfortable seating, and areas designated for relaxation—can enhance comfort and belonging. A welcoming environment signals that the classroom is not solely a place for academic instruction but also a community where every individual is valued.

Integrating social-emotional learning (SEL) into the curriculum enhances a supportive classroom environment by promoting emotional regulation, empathy, and constructive problem-solving. SEL practices like mindfulness exercises, perspective-taking activities, and guided conflict resolution help students develop essential interpersonal and self-regulation skills. Research on the prefrontal cortex and amygdala highlights how repeated engagement in these practices strengthens the brain's capacity for emotional control and decision-making, reinforcing a culture of understanding and connection within the classroom.

Creating a supportive atmosphere requires deliberate and ongoing efforts by educators to build trust, promote inclusivity, design welcoming spaces, and integrate social-emotional learning. Together, these strategies foster an environment where every student feels valued, empowered, and prepared to succeed.

13

Strategies for Differentiated Instruction

In today's diverse classrooms, tailoring lessons to meet the varied needs of students is not just beneficial—it is essential for creating an inclusive learning environment. Recognizing that each student comes with unique backgrounds, learning styles, and abilities enables educators to design lessons that are more effective and engaging. This approach aligns with the principles of differentiated instruction, which emphasize flexibility in teaching methods and materials to accommodate individual differences.

A key strategy for tailoring lessons is employing **multiple means of representation**. Presenting information in various formats—such as visual aids, auditory materials, and hands-on activities—ensures that diverse learning preferences are addressed. For instance, when introducing a complex scientific concept, a teacher might use diagrams, videos, and interactive simulations alongside traditional lectures. This approach supports visual learners, auditory learners, and those who grasp concepts best through kinesthetic experiences, making the material accessible to all.

Another important aspect of tailoring lessons is assessing students' readiness levels and interests before designing instructional plans. **Pre-assessments** provide valuable insights into what students already know and where they may require additional support. For example, if a group of students excels in basic math skills but struggles with word problems, the teacher can focus on strategies to enhance problem-solving abilities rather than revisiting foundational concepts. This targeted approach maximizes instructional time and ensures that lessons meet students where they are at.

Flexible Grouping Techniques

Flexible grouping techniques are an integral component of differentiated instruction, allowing educators to tailor their teaching strategies to meet the diverse needs of students. By organizing groups based on criteria such as skill level, interests, or learning styles, teachers create dynamic classroom environments that foster collaboration, engagement, and personalized learning. This approach enhances academic outcomes while also promoting social interaction and peer support.

One effective method of flexible grouping is the use of **ability-based groups,** where students are grouped according to their proficiency in a specific subject area.

For example, during a reading lesson, students with strong comprehension skills might work together on advanced texts, while those needing additional support focus on simpler materials with guided assistance. This targeted approach ensures that all learners are appropriately challenged and progress at a pace suited to their individual needs, making learning more effective and equitable.

Interest-based grouping is another valuable strategy for fostering engagement and ownership of learning. In this approach, students collaborate on projects or activities aligned with their passions or curiosities. For instance, when studying ecosystems, students might choose to explore different habitats—such as forests, deserts, or oceans—based on their personal interests. This strategy increases motivation and encourages deeper exploration, as students are more likely to invest effort in topics they find meaningful.

Mixed-ability groups are particularly beneficial for promoting peer learning. In these groups, students with varying levels of proficiency collaborate, allowing stronger learners to reinforce their understanding by assisting peers who may need additional support. This model builds confidence in students requiring help while fostering leadership and empathy among more advanced learners. Educators can facilitate effective collaboration within these groups by assigning roles tailored to each student's strengths, ensuring that all members contribute meaningfully to the task.

If you're wondering which grouping strategy to use in your classroom, consider your learning objectives and student needs. Ability-based groups work best for skill-focused instruction, ensuring students receive targeted support or challenges. Interest-based grouping boosts engagement by allowing students to explore topics that spark their curiosity, making it ideal for inquiry-based and creative projects. Mixed-ability groups encourage peer collaboration, leadership, and diverse perspectives, fostering deeper discussions and teamwork. The most effective approach often involves rotating between these strategies to balance individualized instruction with collaborative learning, ensuring all students benefit from varied learning experiences.

To implement flexible grouping effectively, **ongoing assessment** is essential. Teachers should use formative assessments, observations, and student feedback to evaluate progress and adjust group compositions dynamically. Flexibility in grouping allows educators to respond to changing needs, ensuring that instruction remains adaptive, equitable, and aligned with student learning goals.

Adapting Materials for Varied Learners

Adapting materials for varied learners is key for effective differentiated instruction, ensuring that all students have equitable access to meaningful learning opportunities. This process involves modifying content, instructional methods, and assessment strategies to accommodate the diverse needs, interests, and abilities of students in the classroom. Thoughtfully adjusted materials create inclusive learning environments where every student is empowered to succeed.

One effective strategy for adapting materials is the use of **tiered assignments**, which allow educators to present the same core content at varying levels of complexity. For example, when teaching a mathematical concept such as fractions, a teacher might provide straightforward computation problems for students needing foundational support, while offering complex word problems or real-world applications to those ready for advanced challenges. This approach meets learners at their current level while encouraging growth without causing frustration or disengagement.

Tiered assignments ensure that all students engage with the same core content at a level that appropriately challenges them, preventing both frustration and disengagement. Neuroscience research highlights that learning occurs most effectively when tasks are within a student's zone of proximal development—the level at which they can succeed with appropriate support.

When addressing concerns from students, parents, or colleagues, educators can emphasize that differentiation is about fairness, not sameness—every student receives the support or extension they need to build deeper understanding. Aligning tiered assignments with curriculum standards, demonstrating student growth, and explaining that all learners are working toward the same objectives through pathways suited to their cognitive development can reassure stakeholders. Most modern education systems encourage differentiation, but teachers should verify school policies and document their instructional decisions to ensure compliance.

Transparent communication, evidence of effectiveness, and a focus on equitable learning opportunities help build trust and support for tiered instruction.

Incorporating technology provides additional avenues for material adaptation. Digital tools, such as interactive simulations and educational software, enable personalized learning experiences tailored to individual paces and styles. For instance, Platforms like Khan Academy offer adaptive learning paths that adjust based on student performance, ensuring that learners engage with appropriately challenging content while receiving real-time feedback and support. These tools empower students to progress at their own pace, fostering both confidence and competence.

Adapting materials to diverse learning needs requires a combination of digital and visual tools that align with neuroscience principles on memory, attention, and cognitive processing. Interactive educational software and adaptive learning platforms allow students to engage with content at their own pace, reducing cognitive overload and increasing motivation through personalized challenges. At the same time, visual aids such as graphic organizers, infographics, and charts help structure information in a way that supports working memory and comprehension.

Additionally, incorporating alternative formats—such as audio versions of texts or read-aloud strategies—activates multiple sensory pathways, which research suggests can improve retention and engagement. By integrating these strategies, educators create accessible learning environments that cater to different cognitive strengths and learning preferences.

Fostering **student choice** in demonstrating understanding is another critical component of material adaptation. Allowing students to select from various project formats—such as presentations, videos, creative artwork, or written reports—encourages them to engage with content in ways that align with their strengths and interests. This flexibility increases motivation, promotes ownership of the learning process, and fosters creativity and critical thinking.

14

ENHANCING CRITICAL THINKING SKILLS

In every classroom, educators face the challenge of preparing students not just to absorb information, but to question it, analyze it, and apply it in meaningful ways. Critical thinking is the foundation of this process—transforming learners from passive recipients into independent problem-solvers equipped to navigate an increasingly complex world. In an era of rapid information flow, the ability to evaluate sources, reason effectively, and make informed decisions is more important than ever. This chapter explores key strategies for strengthening critical thinking, from inquiry-based learning that fosters curiosity to structured problem-solving frameworks and the careful evaluation of arguments and evidence. By developing these skills, educators empower students to approach challenges with confidence, adaptability, and intellectual independence.

Inquiry-Based Learning

Inquiry-based learning (IBL) is an instructional approach that positions students as active participants in their own learning journey. By encouraging learners to ask questions, explore, and engage deeply with content, IBL shifts the focus from passive information delivery to active discovery. This method not only nurtures curiosity but also enhances critical thinking skills, empowering students to tackle real-world challenges with confidence and creativity.

A core strength of IBL is its ability to foster **higher-order thinking skills**. When students formulate their own questions and investigate solutions, they develop essential analytical and problem-solving abilities. For instance, in a science classroom, students might design experiments based on hypotheses about chemical reactions. This hands-on process reinforces theoretical knowledge in an engaging way.

Inquiry-based learning is strongly supported by neuroscience, as it engages cognitive processes essential for motivation, memory, and deeper learning. When students actively explore concepts and seek answers through meaningful inquiry, they stimulate brain regions linked to curiosity and long-term retention. This approach encourages students to connect new knowledge with prior experiences, reinforcing understanding through active engagement. Additionally, the collaborative nature of IBL enhances learning by promoting peer discussions, which research indicates can strengthen comprehension, increase motivation, and improve problem-solving skills.

By integrating inquiry-based learning into the classroom, educators cultivate an environment where students take ownership of their learning, ask meaningful questions, and develop the skills needed to think critically and adapt to new challenges.

Problem Solving Frameworks

Problem-solving frameworks are essential tools that provide structured methodologies for identifying, analyzing, and resolving challenges effectively. These frameworks guide individuals and teams through the complex problem- solving process, breaking issues into manageable components and encouraging critical thinking. By employing such frameworks, learners can develop a deeper understanding of problem dynamics and improve their decision-making skills.

One widely recognized framework is the **IDEAL model**, which stands for Identify, Define, Explore, Act, and Look Back. This iterative approach begins with identifying the problem clearly, followed by defining its parameters and scope. In the exploration phase, individuals gather relevant information, consider diverse perspectives, and generate potential solutions. The act phase involves implementing the chosen solution, while the final step—looking back— focuses on evaluating outcomes to assess effectiveness and extract lessons for future application. This process enhances critical thinking and builds resilience, as learners adapt their strategies based on feedback and outcomes. For younger students, the IDEAL model can be used in a classroom conflict- resolution activity, where students work through a social disagreement by identifying the issue, discussing possible solutions, and reflecting on how they resolved it. For older students, it can be applied in a debate setting, guiding them through analyzing a complex topic, developing arguments, presenting their case, and evaluating the effectiveness of their reasoning after the discussion.

IDEAL FRAMEWORK

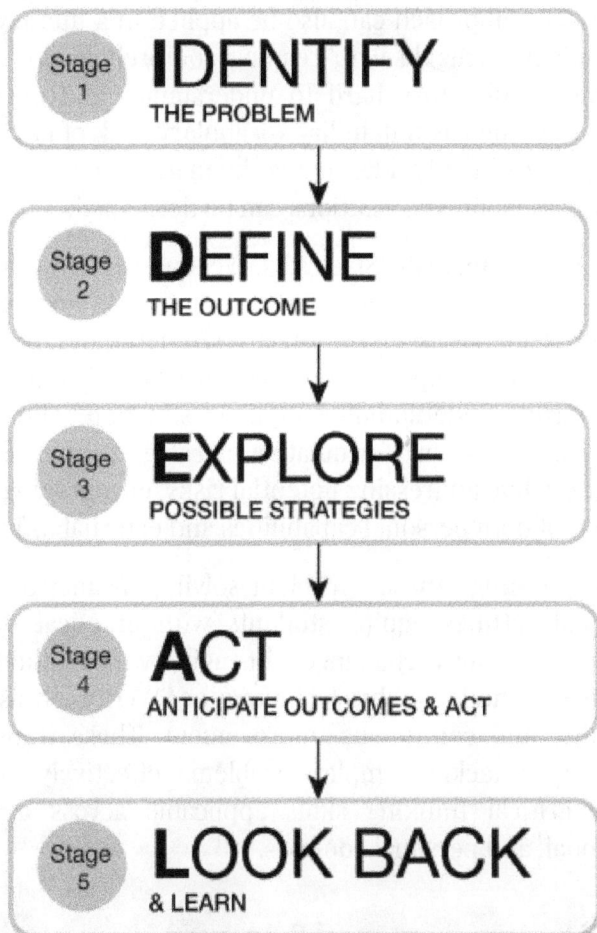

Stage 1 **IDENTIFY**
THE PROBLEM

Stage 2 **DEFINE**
THE OUTCOME

Stage 3 **EXPLORE**
POSSIBLE STRATEGIES

Stage 4 **ACT**
ANTICIPATE OUTCOMES & ACT

Stage 5 **LOOK BACK**
& LEARN

Another effective method is the **5 Whys technique**, which emphasizes root cause analysis by asking "why" repeatedly until the core issue is uncovered. This approach prevents superficial solutions and promotes deep inquiry. For example, in an IT class, the 5 Whys technique can be used to troubleshoot a coding error—

beginning with 'Why isn't the program running?' and drilling down into issues like syntax errors, incorrect logic, missing dependencies, or deeper gaps in understanding programming concepts. This approach can also be applied in a literacy lesson when students struggle with reading comprehension—starting with 'Why is this story hard to understand?' and uncovering deeper issues such as unfamiliar vocabulary, lack of background knowledge, or difficulty identifying the main idea. By addressing root causes, sustainable solutions can be developed.

The **SWOT analysis** (Strengths, Weaknesses, Opportunities, Threats) is another well-known framework for strategic problem-solving. By assessing internal strengths and weaknesses alongside external opportunities and threats, individuals gain a comprehensive understanding of their situation. This holistic perspective helps in formulating strategies that leverage advantages while addressing potential risks, encouraging critical evaluation of both personal capabilities and external influences.

Incorporating these problem-solving frameworks into educational settings equips students with practical tools for navigating real-world challenges. Engaging with methodologies like the IDEAL model, 5 Whys technique, or SWOT analysis fosters adaptability and continuous improvement. These frameworks help students tackle complex problems effectively and also cultivate critical thinking skills applicable across academic, professional, and personal contexts.

Evaluating Arguments and Evidence

Evaluating arguments and evidence is an important part of critical thinking, enabling individuals to assess the validity, reliability, and relevance of information presented in support of a claim. Mastering this skill is essential for discerning between well-founded arguments and those that are misleading or fallacious, ultimately leading to more informed and rational decision-making.

A foundational step in evaluating arguments is understanding their structure, which typically includes premises that support a conclusion. To assess an argument effectively, it is important to identify these components clearly. For instance, in a debate about climate change policies, recognizing the premises—such as data on rising global temperatures—and how they connect to the conclusion advocating for policy changes is critical. This clarity provides the basis for examining the strength of the argument. For primary school teachers, teaching argument evaluation can begin with simple activities like having students compare two versions of a story to identify which is more believable and why. Encouraging young learners to ask, "How do we know this is true?" when reading books, watching videos, or discussing classroom topics helps them develop early critical thinking skills in an age-appropriate way.

Examining the **quality of evidence** is equally crucial. Not all evidence carries the same weight, and assessing its credibility, relevance, and context is vital. For example, Peer-reviewed studies from reputable sources provide more robust support than anecdotal claims or unverified online information. Additionally, engaging with diverse perspectives and sources can help mitigate personal biases and provide a broader understanding of complex issues. Neuroscience research suggests that cognitive biases—such as confirmation bias—stem from the brain's tendency to favor familiar or emotionally reinforcing information. Teaching students to slow down their reasoning, compare multiple sources, and actively question assumptions helps counteract these automatic mental shortcuts.

For younger students, a practical exercise might involve presenting two different accounts of the same event and guiding a discussion on how perspectives shape the way information is presented.

Identifying logical fallacies is another essential aspect of evaluating arguments. Logical fallacies, such as ad hominem attacks (criticizing the person instead of the argument) or straw man arguments (misrepresenting an opponent's position), undermine an argument's validity. Recognizing these errors sharpens critical thinking and equips individuals to engage more constructively in discussions by focusing on the argument's substance rather than its flaws.

Using structured approaches like the **Toulmin model** can further enhance the evaluation process. This framework breaks down arguments into components: claim (the main assertion), grounds (evidence), warrant (the reasoning linking evidence to the claim), backing (additional support for the warrant), rebuttal (counter-arguments), and qualifier (the strength of the claim). By analyzing each part systematically, learners gain a deeper understanding of the argument and its nuances, enabling more thorough evaluations.

Developing the ability to evaluate arguments and evidence is an essential skill for navigating today's complex information landscape. By understanding argument structures, assessing evidence quality, identifying logical fallacies, and applying systematic approaches, individuals enhance their critical thinking abilities and contribute meaningfully to discourse in academic, professional, and personal contexts.

15

THE ROLE OF PLAY IN LEARNING

Play-based learning is a dynamic and effective approach that leverages the natural curiosity of children to foster cognitive, social, and emotional development. This method bridges the gap between unstructured exploration and structured education, promoting engagement while cultivating critical thinking, creativity, and problem-solving skills. By integrating play into learning, educators can create environments that support holistic growth.

The significance of play-based learning lies in its alignment with how children naturally acquire knowledge. Through exploration and interaction, children actively construct understanding rather than passively absorbing information. For example, role-playing scenarios enable children to practice language skills, develop empathy by assuming different perspectives, and engage in collaboration with peers—essential components of social development. These activities make learning enjoyable and provide opportunities for practicing real-world skills in a safe and supportive context.

Neuroscience research underscores the importance of play-based learning for students of all ages by highlighting its impact on brain development. Playful activities stimulate neural pathways associated with memory retention, cognitive flexibility, and creativity. For example, building with blocks or participating in imaginative games activates brain regions responsible for spatial awareness, problem-solving, and innovative thinking. This kind of engagement ensures that learning is not only hands-on but also deeply embedded in the brain's development processes.

Incorporating play into educational settings requires thoughtful planning to balance spontaneity with curricular objectives. For instance, a science lesson might involve an interactive experiment where students hypothesize outcomes based on observations made during play. This inquiry-based approach allows questions to emerge organically, driven by the student's interests, while still achieving key learning goals. Similarly, math concepts can be explored through games or manipulatives, making abstract ideas more concrete and accessible.

Understanding play-based learning also involves recognizing its role in nurturing a love for learning. By valuing play alongside traditional teaching methods, educators create an environment where curiosity and exploration thrive. This approach supports the development of essential academic skills and also fosters resilience, adaptability, and intrinsic motivation.

Play-based learning is more than just a tool for early childhood education; it is a foundational element in fostering holistic development. By integrating play thoughtfully into teaching practices, educators can enhance engagement, reinforce cognitive and social skills.

One effective way to integrate play into the curriculum is through **thematic units** that connect various subjects around a central theme. For example, a unit on "Community Helpers" might include role-playing activities where students act as firefighters, doctors, or teachers. These activities make learning enjoyable while supporting children to practice language skills, develop empathy, and gain a deeper understanding of societal roles. By weaving play into such themes, educators can create interdisciplinary lessons that are both meaningful and engaging.

Outdoor play and nature-based activities further enhance learning by connecting classroom concepts with real-world experiences. For instance, scavenger hunts or nature walks encourage exploration and observation, making subjects like science and geography tangible. While examining a garden, students can discuss plant biology, ecosystems, and environmental stewardship, building a hands-on understanding of abstract ideas. These experiences also nurture a sense of wonder about the natural world, reinforcing concepts in an impactful way.

Technology provides additional opportunities to incorporate play into the curriculum. Digital games and interactive applications allow students to engage with subjects like math, literacy, or coding in an exciting and collaborative manner. For instance, gamified educational apps can encourage problem-solving and teamwork, blending entertainment with academic growth. The use of technology broadens the scope of playful learning whilst meeting the needs of tech-savvy learners in modern classrooms.

Successful incorporation of play requires educators to adopt a flexible mindset that values both spontaneity and structure.

Observing students' interests and adapting activities accordingly ensures lessons remain relevant and engaging. Playful learning environments foster student agency, allowing students to take ownership of their educational journey while cultivating intrinsic motivation.

A significant contribution of play to cognitive development is its enhancement of executive functions, which include working memory, cognitive flexibility, and inhibitory control. In activities such as pretend play or games that require turn- taking help, children practice managing their thoughts and actions. For instance, during role-playing scenarios—such as pretending to run a store or reenacting a story—children plan and organize their actions while navigating social dynamics. This type of imaginative play encourages them to consider different perspectives, evaluate outcomes, and adapt their thinking, fostering critical and flexible thought processes.

Play also has an important role in **language development**, as it provides rich contexts for communication. Collaborative games and group activities prompt students to express their ideas, negotiate rules, and articulate emotions. These interactions expand vocabulary, strengthen comprehension, and develop active listening skills. For example, games like "Simon Says" introduce new vocabulary and reinforce listening skills in a playful and engaging way. This interactive aspect of play ensures that language development occurs naturally within meaningful social interactions. Additionally, the exploration and curiosity inherent in play promote cognitive growth. Open-ended activities—such as building with blocks, conducting simple science experiments, or exploring nature—encourage children to ask questions, test hypotheses, and learn through trial and error. This inquiry-driven approach nurtures a love for learning by allowing children to actively engage with their environment and discover answers independently, reinforcing their problem-solving abilities and intellectual curiosity.

Play is a powerful catalyst for cognitive development, providing a dynamic platform for students to build essential skills in a supportive and engaging environment. By incorporating play into educational settings—whether through structured games or unstructured exploration—educators can create opportunities for intellectual growth while ensuring that the learning process remains enjoyable and enriching.

16

STRESS MANAGEMENT TECHNIQUES FOR EDUCATORS

Understanding the sources of teacher stress is essential for developing effective strategies to support educators' well-being. Teachers face a unique set of challenges that can lead to emotional and physical strain, ultimately affecting their personal health and professional effectiveness. By identifying these stressors, educators and school administrators can implement proactive measures to mitigate their effects and create a healthier, more sustainable work environment. This topic was highlighted in Chapter 5, and the current chapter will delve deeper specifically into stress management techniques for teachers.

A primary source of teacher stress is the overwhelming workload. Lesson planning, grading, administrative duties, and meeting curriculum standards often require long hours beyond the classroom. These demands are intensified by the need to provide differentiated instruction for diverse student needs, which adds complexity and time to an already packed schedule. This relentless workload can lead to burnout, as educators struggle to balance professional responsibilities with personal well-being.

Classroom management is another significant stressor. Managing disruptive behaviors, addressing disengaged students, and maintaining an orderly learning environment can be emotionally draining. When teachers encounter ongoing challenges in discipline or student engagement, they may experience feelings of inadequacy or frustration. This stress is further compounded by demands for accountability from parents and administrators, which can create an atmosphere of constant scrutiny and pressure. Neuroscience research suggests that prolonged exposure to stress activates the amygdala, the brain's emotional processing center, while impairing functions of the prefrontal cortex, which is responsible for decision-making and impulse control. This can make it more difficult for teachers to regulate emotions, respond calmly to classroom disruptions, and maintain focus, ultimately leading to increased burnout and reduced effectiveness in managing student behavior.

The emotional toll of teaching can also contribute to stress. Teachers often form deep connections with their students, which makes them emotionally invested in their well-being. While these relationships can be rewarding, they also expose educators to secondary trauma or distress when students face personal challenges such as mental health issues, or family instability. Balancing the dual roles of educator and emotional support provider can place an immense burden on teachers' mental health.

External factors such as limited resources, insufficient administrative support, and unrealistic societal expectations further exacerbate teacher stress levels. Teachers often feel the weight of working within systems that lack adequate funding or fail to prioritize their professional development and well-being. Recognizing these stressors is the first step toward implementing targeted interventions—whether through wellness initiatives, professional development focused on classroom management, or systemic changes aimed at reducing workloads and improving support structures.

Self-care practices are vital for educators to maintain their well-being and sustain their effectiveness in the classroom. Teaching comes with unique challenges, and prioritizing self-care can significantly reduce stress, improve mental health, and enhance job satisfaction. By incorporating intentional self- care routines, educators can build resilience and create a positive, balanced approach to both their personal and professional lives.

One essential self-care practice is **establishing clear boundaries** between work and personal life. Teachers often extend their work hours into evenings and weekends, leading to burnout and diminished energy. Setting specific times to disconnect from work-related tasks allows educators to recharge mentally and physically. For instance, designating evenings or weekends as "no work" time enables teachers to focus on hobbies, spend quality time with family and friends, or simply relax. This balance fosters rejuvenation and prevents work from overshadowing personal well-being.

Mindfulness techniques also play a crucial role in educator self-care. Incorporating practices such as meditation, deep breathing, or guided visualization into daily routines can help reduce anxiety and enhance emotional regulation. Even brief mindfulness sessions—such as five minutes of focused breathing during a break—can offer significant relief from daily stressors.

Schools can support these efforts by offering mindfulness workshops or creating quiet spaces where teachers can practice mindfulness during the day.

Another critical component of self-care is **physical activity**, which benefits both physical and mental health. Regular exercise releases endorphins that improve mood, alleviate stress, and boost energy levels. Simple activities, such as a brisk walk during lunch breaks, yoga sessions, or participation in after-school fitness programs, can be integrated into busy schedules to promote well-being. Making time for movement ensures that educators stay physically energized and mentally refreshed.

Building supportive relationships with colleagues can also enhance self-care efforts by providing a sense of camaraderie and shared understanding. A strong network of peers offers an outlet for sharing experiences, exchanging coping strategies, and providing mutual encouragement. Collaborative planning sessions, peer mentorship programs, or informal gatherings can strengthen these connections while fostering a sense of community within the school environment.

Prioritizing self-care is essential for educators to navigate the demands of teaching successfully. By setting boundaries, practicing mindfulness, staying physically active, and cultivating supportive relationships, teachers can safeguard their well-being, improve their resilience, and maintain a healthy work-life balance that ultimately benefits both themselves and their students.

Work Life Balance

Creating a balanced work-life approach is essential for educators, who often face the demands of extended hours spent on lesson planning, grading, and administrative responsibilities. Without a structured balance, these demands can encroach on personal time, leading to burnout and diminished effectiveness. A well-rounded approach enhances personal well-being and also improves professional performance, benefiting both teachers and their students.

A key strategy for achieving balance is the implementation of time management techniques. Educators can prioritize tasks using tools such as the Eisenhower Matrix, which categorizes tasks into urgent and important, non-urgent but important, and so forth. By focusing on high-priority responsibilities during the school day, teachers can create space in their schedules for personal pursuits and relaxation in the evenings and on weekends.

Leveraging technology is another effective way to streamline tasks and enhance productivity. Digital tools such as planners, task management apps, and automated grading systems enable educators to organize schedules, set reminders, and track progress. For example, task management platforms like Trello or Google Calendar can consolidate deadlines and plans, freeing up mental energy and time for self-care or family activities. By optimizing workflows through technology, educators can achieve greater efficiency and reclaim valuable personal time.

Fostering a supportive school culture also plays a vital role in achieving work- life balance. Open communication among staff about workload challenges can reduce feelings of isolation and promote collaboration. Administrators can support this balance by providing resources such as counselling services, wellness initiatives, or professional development focused on stress management. When educators feel supported by their colleagues and administration, they are more likely to maintain a sustainable balance and prioritize their well-being.

Engaging in hobbies and personal interests outside of teaching further enriches a balanced lifestyle. Creative outlets such as painting, gardening, or playing music offer a refreshing escape from work-related stress and contribute to personal fulfillment. These activities provide a sense of purpose beyond professional responsibilities, enhancing overall happiness and resilience.

17

COMMUNITY ENGAGEMENT AND SUPPORT

Education does not exist in isolation - it thrives through strong connections between schools, families, and the broader community. When students see that their learning extends beyond the classroom, they become more engaged, motivated, and prepared for real-world challenges. Meaningful partnerships with families, collaboration with local organizations, and opportunities for student advocacy create a supportive network that enriches both academic and personal growth. This chapter explores how fostering these relationships strengthens education, ensuring that students are not only supported in their learning but also empowered to shape their own futures. By building a culture of shared responsibility, schools can transform from institutions of instruction into vibrant hubs of collaboration and opportunity.

Building Partnerships with Families

Building partnerships with families is a fundamental component of effective community engagement in education. Strong family-school relationships enhance student learning and foster a supportive environment where parents and guardians feel valued and involved. By collaborating with families, educators can adopt a holistic approach to education that recognizes the critical role families play in their children's academic and personal success.

A key strategy for building these partnerships is regular and transparent communication. Schools can utilize a variety of platforms—such as newsletters, email updates, social media, and parent-teacher conferences—to keep families informed about school activities, curriculum updates, and their child's progress. Open and consistent communication builds trust and encourages families to actively engage in their child's educational journey. For example, sending regular progress reports or classroom updates ensures that parents are well-informed and can support their children at home.

Another effective approach is hosting workshops or informational sessions tailored to empower families with the knowledge and tools needed to support their children's learning. Sessions on topics such as effective homework routines, understanding developmental milestones, or navigating technology in education equip parents with practical strategies to assist their children. These initiatives strengthen family-school collaboration and also underscores the school's commitment to supporting families as partners in education.

Creating opportunities for family participation in school activities is equally vital. Events such as open houses, cultural celebrations, or volunteer days provide families with opportunities to connect with teachers, staff, and other parents while fostering a sense of belonging within the school community. Active family involvement in school events promotes stronger parental investment in education and helps cultivate a positive school culture.

Additionally, recognizing and respecting the diverse backgrounds and perspectives of families is essential. Understanding cultural differences allows educators to communicate effectively and create an inclusive environment that values every family's unique contribution. By embracing diversity and being responsive to families' needs, schools can ensure that all families feel welcome and supported in their efforts to help their children succeed.

Involving Community Resources

Involving community resources is an essential component of creating a well- rounded educational environment that extends learning beyond the classroom. By collaborating with local organizations, businesses, and volunteers, schools can provide students with enriched learning opportunities and real-world experiences. This approach benefits students, strengthens community bonds, and promotes a shared commitment to education.

One effective strategy for integrating community resources is through partnerships with local businesses. These collaborations can result in internship programs, mentorship opportunities, or specialized workshops that equip students with practical skills and insights into potential career paths. For example, a local technology company might offer coding workshops for high school students, providing hands-on experience in a rapidly evolving field. Such initiatives prepare students for future employment while fostering connections between schools and the local economy. Engaging non-profit organizations is another impactful way to enhance educational experiences. Many non-profits bring specialized expertise and resources that can support specific subjects. For instance, environmental organizations might partner with schools to conduct outdoor learning activities focused on sustainability and conservation. These partnerships have the potential to provide unique learning opportunities and inspire students to take an active role in addressing societal challenges.

Local cultural institutions—such as museums, libraries, and theaters—can also serve as valuable educational partners. Collaborations with these institutions can make learning more dynamic and interactive. For example, field trips to a museum can deepen students' understanding of historical or scientific concepts, while partnerships with a theater group can enhance creative expression through drama workshops. Schools might even co-create exhibits or performances with these institutions, allowing students to showcase their knowledge and creativity while engaging with the broader community.

Finally, schools should actively encourage volunteerism among parents and community members. Structured volunteer programs enable individuals to contribute their time and skills effectively, creating stronger ties between families, schools, and the local community. Volunteers can support initiatives such as tutoring programs, organizing events like science fairs, or mentoring students in extracurricular activities. These contributions enrich the educational experience while fostering a sense of community ownership in student success.

Promoting Student Advocacy

Promoting student advocacy is an essential step in empowering learners to actively participate in shaping their educational experiences and expressing their needs within the school community. By fostering a culture of empowerment, schools enable students to become confident, responsible, and engaged individuals. This enhances personal development and contributes to a more inclusive and responsive educational system. Neuroscience research suggests that when students have a sense of control over their learning, it activates regions of the brain associated with motivation and reward processing. This engagement not only enhances their ability to advocate for themselves but also strengthens their resilience and problem-solving skills, preparing them to navigate challenges both in and beyond the classroom.

One of the most effective strategies for encouraging student advocacy is the establishment of student councils or representative bodies. These organizations provide students with a structured platform to voice their opinions on matters ranging from academic policies to extracurricular activities. A well-organized student council fosters open dialogue between students and school leadership, ensuring that the perspectives of the student body are considered in decision- making processes. This engagement amplifies student voices and also deepens educators' understanding of the challenges their learners face, enabling more informed and inclusive policy development.

Integrating advocacy training into the curriculum equips students with critical skills such as public speaking, negotiation, and problem-solving. Workshops, seminars, or guest speakers—such as community leaders or experienced advocates—can inspire students to become change agents within their schools.

For example, initiatives that focus on social justice issues encourage students to identify problems within their communities and develop actionable solutions. This hands-on approach reinforces the importance of civic engagement and demonstrates how advocacy can drive meaningful change.

Creating peer mentorship programs is another powerful way to support student advocacy. By pairing younger students with experienced advocates, schools provide a space for knowledge-sharing and skill development. Mentorship builds confidence among mentees and creates a supportive network that facilitates ongoing dialogue about key issues affecting the student body. This collaborative dynamic helps ensure that advocacy efforts remain sustainable and impactful over time.

Additionally, schools can leverage technology and digital platforms to expand the reach of student advocacy. Encouraging students to use social media responsibly allows them to raise awareness about causes they are passionate about and connect with broader communities. Digital campaigns and online initiatives provide students with an opportunity to amplify their voices beyond the school environment, inspiring collective action and fostering a sense of global citizenship.

18

FUTURE TRENDS IN EDUCATIONAL NEUROSCIENCE

The future of education is unfolding, and educators are at the forefront of this transformation. As neuroscience continues to reveal how the brain learns best, teachers have an unprecedented opportunity to apply these insights in ways that enhance student engagement, deepen understanding, and make learning more meaningful. The next era of education is not about replacing traditional teaching methods but refining them—leveraging cutting-edge research to create classrooms where every student can thrive.

The field of educational neuroscience is evolving rapidly, with groundbreaking research offering deeper insights into how students learn. These advancements extend beyond theory, providing practical applications that enhance classroom instruction and have the potential to improve student outcomes. As neuroscience continues to uncover the brain's learning mechanisms, educators can align their teaching practices with evidence-based strategies to maximize engagement, retention, and critical thinking. Emerging innovations in artificial intelligence (AI), connectomics, neurotechnology, cognitive flexibility training, and personalized learning models are shaping the future of education, offering new possibilities for both students and teachers.

Artificial Intelligence (AI) in Adaptive Learning

One transformative area of exploration is artificial intelligence (AI) in adaptive learning. AI-powered learning platforms use real-time data to analyze student performance, adjusting instructional content based on individual progress. Unlike traditional methods, these systems personalize learning experiences by identifying areas where students need additional support or challenge. AI-driven adaptive learning systems align with cognitive science principles by dynamically adjusting instructional content based on student progress, reinforcing learning through timely review cycles and differentiated instruction.

For younger students, AI-driven educational games like DreamBox Learning adjust difficulty levels dynamically, keeping engagement high while building foundational skills. For older students, Carnegie Learning's MATHia provides AI-driven problem-solving support, offering real-time feedback that enhances metacognitive awareness and self-directed learning. Beyond educational games, AI-powered adaptive tutoring systems are enabling real-time assessment and personalized feedback, enhancing instructional precision.

Connectomics and the Future of Personalized Learning

Another promising development is connectomics—the study of how neurons in the brain are wired together, helping researchers understand how information is processed, stored, and recalled. While still in early research phases, connectomics aims to map neural connectivity to better understand cognitive processing. Think of your brain like a giant city with millions of roads connecting different places. These roads (called neural connections) allow information to travel from one part of your brain to another. Connectomics is like making a map of all these roads. Scientists want to understand which roads exist (how neurons are connected), how traffic flows (how information moves between brain areas) and what happens if a road is blocked (how learning difficulties or brain injuries affect thinking) By mapping these connections, researchers hope to figure out how different people learn, remember, and solve problems—which could one day help teachers personalize lessons based on how a student's brain works best. Although its direct applications in differentiated instruction remain speculative, ongoing research suggests that future insights could contribute to a deeper understanding of individual learning variability.

Future advancements may allow AI-driven tools to leverage connectomics- informed models, enabling more personalized learning pathways. However, practical classroom applications remain largely theoretical at this stage.

Neurotechnology's Expanding Role in Education

Neurotechnology's role in education is also expanding. Tools such as EEG (electroencephalography) and functional near-infrared spectroscopy (fNIRS) allow researchers to monitor attention and engagement patterns during learning. While these tools do not measure cognitive load directly, they track neural markers of engagement, working memory demands, and attentional fluctuations, providing insights into how students focus and process information during learning.

Educators can use research from these studies to optimize instructional pacing and activity structure. Additionally, brain-computer interfaces (BCIs) show promise for students with disabilities, offering potential real-time interventions to support working memory, executive function, and attention regulation. While BCIs are still in development, early research indicates their potential to enhance executive function, attention regulation, and assistive communication, improving accessibility for neurodiverse learners.

Cognitive Flexibility Training and Problem-Solving Skills

A growing area of focus in educational neuroscience is cognitive flexibility training, which enhances students' ability to adapt, switch perspectives, and solve novel problems. Research suggests that cognitive flexibility involves a network of brain regions, primarily **the prefrontal cortex, anterior cingulate cortex (ACC), and parietal lobes**, which regulate adaptive thinking, task switching, and response inhibition.

Schools are beginning to integrate activities such as multimodal problem- solving, interdisciplinary projects, and reflective metacognition exercises to strengthen these skills. For a primary school teacher, this means incorporating activities like open-ended storytelling, collaborative puzzles, or switching between different ways to solve math problems, helping young learners practice thinking flexibly and approaching challenges from multiple angles. Encouraging students to engage with diverse perspectives, debate contrasting viewpoints, and apply knowledge across subjects fosters adaptability—an essential skill for success in an unpredictable world.

KEY BRAIN REGIONS FOR COGNITIVE FLEXIBILITY

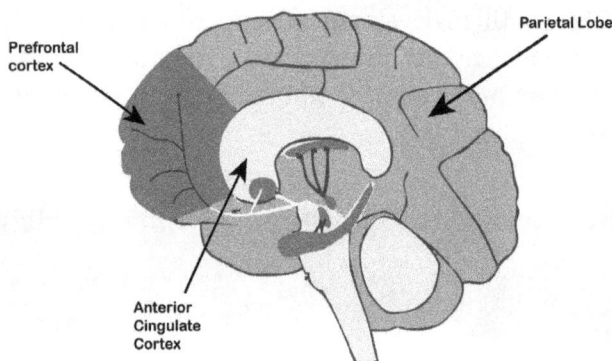

Prefrontal cortex

Parietal Lobe

Anterior Cingulate Cortex

The Rise of Personalized Learning Models

Personalized learning models are also gaining traction, using insights from neuroscience to create more responsive, flexible instruction. Neuroscience research on cognitive diversity highlights the importance of designing adaptable learning environments that provide multiple ways for students to engage with content, avoiding rigid one-size-fits-all approaches.

Personalized learning models leverage structured autonomy, integrating diverse instructional strategies that allow students to engage with content through flexible, adaptable pathways that support both guided instruction and independent exploration. By integrating strategies such as inquiry-based learning, project-based exploration, and adaptive feedback, educators can balance autonomy with structured support, fostering deeper engagement and long-term knowledge retention.

Preparing Educators for Change

With rapid advancements in neuroscience and technology, preparing educators for change is critical to ensuring that these insights translate into effective teaching practices. Teachers could benefit from access to professional development programs that bridge neuroscience research with practical classroom strategies. Training should emphasize how the brain processes, retains, and applies information, providing educators with evidence-based tools to enhance student engagement and learning outcomes.

Collaborative professional learning communities provide another valuable approach for integrating neuroscience-based strategies into classrooms. Schools can establish peer mentorship programs, where experienced educators guide colleagues in implementing brain-informed practices. Classroom observations, co-teaching models, and collaborative lesson planning offer opportunities for teachers to witness neuroscience-based strategies in action, fostering continuous professional growth.

Technology also plays a growing role in educator training. AI-powered coaching tools, VR training simulations, and interactive neuroscience courses now offer teachers immersive, hands-on learning experiences. For example, simulated classroom scenarios allow educators to practice managing cognitive load, implementing scaffolding techniques, and adapting instruction for students with diverse learning needs—all within a controlled, data-driven environment.

Engaging parents, administrators, and policymakers is equally important in sustaining these changes. Schools can offer neuroscience-informed workshops for parents, equipping them with strategies to support cognitive development at home, such as optimizing sleep hygiene, managing stress, and fostering curiosity through play-based learning. Meanwhile, school administrators can use data-driven insights from neuroscience to inform policies that prioritize equity, inclusion, and evidence-based instructional design—ensuring that learning environments are tailored to the diverse needs of all students.

The future of education will be defined by those who embrace change, not as a challenge but as an opportunity to create better learning experiences for every student. Neuroscience provides invaluable insights into how the brain learns, but these insights are only as powerful as their application in the classroom. Educators are not just recipients of this knowledge—they are the catalysts for transforming it into meaningful practice. By integrating neuroscience-driven strategies, adapting to emerging technologies, and fostering environments that support diverse learning needs, teachers can shape an educational landscape that is more engaging, equitable, and effective. The science is clear: when we teach in ways that align with how the brain learns best, we empower not just students but entire generations to think critically, solve problems, and thrive in an ever-evolving world.

REFERENCES

- Bandura, A. (1997). Self-Efficacy: The Exercise of Control. Freeman.

- Ansari, D., Coch, D. (2006). "Bridges over troubled waters: Education and cognitive neuroscience." *Trends in Cognitive Sciences*, 10(4), 146–151.

- Goswami, U. (2006). "Neuroscience and education: from research to practice?" *Nature Reviews Neuroscience*, 7(5), 406–413.

- Howard-Jones, P. (2014). Neuroscience and Education: A Review of Educational Interventions and Approaches Informed by Neuroscience. Education Endowment Foundation.

- Johnson, M. H. (2001). "Functional brain development in humans." *Nature Reviews Neuroscience*, 2(7), 475–483.

- Casey, B. J., Tottenham, N., Liston, C., Durston, S. (2005). "Imaging the developing brain: what have we learned about cognitive development?" *Trends in Cognitive Sciences*, 9(3), 104–110.

- Blakemore, S. J., Frith, U. (2005). *The Learning Brain: Lessons for Education.* Blackwell Publishing.

- Squire, L. R., Zola-Morgan, S. (1991). "The medial temporal lobe memory system." *Science*, 253(5026), 1380–1386.

- Eichenbaum, H. (2000). "A cortical-hippocampal system for declarative memory." *Nature Reviews Neuroscience*, 1(1), 41–50.

- Baddeley, A. (2000). "The episodic buffer: a new component of working memory?" *Trends in Cognitive Sciences*, 4(11), 417–423.

- Posner, M. I., Petersen, S. E. (1990). "The attention system of the human brain." *Annual Review of Neuroscience*, 13(1), 25–42.

- Diamond, A. (2013). "Executive functions." *Annual Review of Psychology*, 64, 135–168.

- Barkley, R. A. (1997). "Behavioral inhibition, sustained attention, and executive functions: constructing a unifying theory of ADHD." *Psychological Bulletin*, 121(1), 65–94.

- Kuhl, P. K. (2004). "Early language acquisition: cracking the speech code." *Nature Reviews Neuroscience*, 5(11), 831–843.

- Friederici, A. D. (2002). "Towards a neural basis of auditory sentence processing." *Trends in Cognitive Sciences*, 6(2), 78–84.

- Neville, H. J., Bavelier, D. (1998). "Neural organization and plasticity of language." *Current Opinion in Neurobiology*, 8(2), 254–258.

- Shaywitz, S. E., Shaywitz, B. A., Pugh, K. R., et al. (1998). "Functional disruption in the organization of the brain for reading in dyslexia." *Proceedings of the National Academy of Sciences*, 95(5), 2636–2641.

- Snowling, M. J. (2000). *Dyslexia*. Blackwell Publishing.

- Dehaene, S., Cohen, L. (1995). "Towards an anatomical and functional model of number processing." *Mathematical Cognition*, 1(1), 83–120.

- Butterworth, B. (1999). *The Mathematical Brain.* Macmillan.

- Greenberg, M. T., Weissberg, R. P., O'Brien, M. U., et al. (2003). "Enhancing school-based prevention and youth development through coordinated social, emotional, and academic learning." *American Psychologist*, 58(6-7), 466–474.

- Denham, S. A., Brown, C. (2010). "Plays nice with others: Social–emotional learning and academic success." *Early Education and Development*, 21(5), 652–680.

- Ryan, R. M., Deci, E. L. (2000). "Intrinsic and extrinsic motivations: Classic definitions and new directions." *Contemporary Educational Psychology*, 25(1), 54–67.

- Panksepp, J. (1998). Affective Neuroscience: The Foundations of Human and Animal Emotions. Oxford University Press.

- Berridge, K. C., Robinson, T. E. (2003). "Parsing reward." *Trends in Neurosciences*, 26(9), 507–513.

- McEwen, B. S. (2000). "The neurobiology of stress: from serendipity to clinical relevance." *Brain Research*, 886(1-2), 172–189.

- Lupien, S. J., McEwen, B. S., Gunnar, M. R., Heim, C. (2009). "Effects of stress throughout the lifespan on the brain, behaviour and cognition." *Nature Reviews Neuroscience*, 10(6), 434–445.

- Hattie, J., Timperley, H. (2007). "The Power of Feedback." *Review of Educational Research*, 77(1), 81–112.

- Goleman, D. (1995). Emotional Intelligence: Why It Can Matter More Than IQ. Bantam Books.

- Vygotsky, L. S. (1978). Mind in Society: The Development of Higher Psychological Processes. Harvard University Press.

- Wiggins, G., McTighe, J. (2005). *Understanding by Design.* ASCD.

- Kahneman, D. (2011). *Thinking, Fast and Slow.* Farrar, Straus and Giroux.

- Brown, S. (2009). Play: How It Shapes the Brain, Opens the Imagination, and Invigorates the Soul. Avery.

- Sawyer, R. K. (2014). *The Cambridge Handbook of the Learning Sciences* (2nd ed.). Cambridge University Press.

- Holmes, W., Bialik, M., Fadel, C. (2019). Artificial Intelligence in Education: Promises and Implications for Teaching and Learning. Center for Curriculum Redesign.

- Mason, L. (2009). "Bridging Neuroscience and Education: A Two-Way Path is Possible?" *Mind, Brain, and Education*, 3(1), 35–49.

- Zull, J. E. (2011). The Brain, the Mind, and the Classroom: The Science of Learning. Stylus Publishing.

- Mayer, R. E. (2009). *Multimedia Learning* (2nd ed.). Cambridge University Press.

- Duckworth, A. (2016). Grit: The Power of Passion and Perseverance. Scribner.

- Dweck, C. S. (2006). Mindset: The New Psychology of Success. Random House.

- Brackett, M. A. (2019). Permission to Feel: Unlocking the Power of Emotions to Help Our Kids, Ourselves, and Our Society Thrive. Celadon Books.

- Carew, T. J., Magsamen, S. (2010). "Neuroscience and education: An ideal partnership for producing evidence-based solutions to guide 21st-century learning." *Neuron*, 67(5), 685–688.

- Gazzaniga, M. S., Ivry, R. B., Mangun, G. R. (2018). *Cognitive Neuroscience: The Biology of the Mind* (5th ed.). W.W. Norton & Company.

- Koizumi, H. (2004). "The concept of 'developing the brain': A new natural science for learning and education." *Brain and Development*, 26(7), 434–441.

- Sweller, J., Ayres, P., Kalyuga, S. (2011). *Cognitive Load Theory*. Springer.

- Kirschner, P. A., Sweller, J., Clark, R. E. (2006). "Why minimal guidance during instruction does not work: An analysis of the failure of constructivist, discovery, problem-based, experiential, and inquiry-based teaching." *Educational Psychologist*, 41(2), 75–86.

- Meltzoff, A. N., Kuhl, P. K., Movellan, J., Sejnowski, T. J. (2009). "Foundations for a new science of learning." *Science*, 325(5938), 284–288.

- Bransford, J. D., Schwartz, D. L. (1999). "Rethinking transfer: A simple proposal with multiple implications." *Review of Research in Education*, 24, 61–100.

- Sousa, D. A. (2017). *How the Brain Learns Mathematics* (2nd ed.). Corwin Press.

- Hinton, C., Miyamoto, K., Della-Chiesa, B. (2008). "Brain research, learning and emotions: implications for education research, policy and practice." *European Journal of Education*, 43(1), 87–103.

- Pinker, S. (1997). *How the Mind Works.* W.W. Norton & Company.

- Geary, D. C. (2011). "Cognitive predictors of achievement growth in mathematics: A five-year longitudinal study." *Developmental Psychology*, 47(6), 1539–1552.

- Siegler, R. S., Lortie-Forgues, H. (2015). "Conceptual knowledge of fractions and decimals." *Educational Psychologist*, 50(1), 38–59.

- Hirsh-Pasek, K., Golinkoff, R. M. (2011). "The great balancing act: Optimizing brain development and learning in early childhood." *Journal of Neuroscience & Education*, 12(3), 95–101.

- Keller, J. M. (2010). Motivational Design for Learning and Performance: The ARCS Model Approach. Springer.

- Tomasello, M. (1999). *The Cultural Origins of Human Cognition.* Harvard University Press.

- Dolan, R. J., Dayan, P. (2013). "Goals and habits in the brain." *Neuron*, 80(2), 312–325.

- Fischer, K. W., Bidell, T. R. (2006). "Dynamic development of action, thought, and emotion." In R. M. Lerner & W. Damon (Eds.), *Handbook of Child Psychology: Theoretical Models of Human Development* (6th ed., Vol. 1, pp. 313–399). Wiley.

- Hattie, J. (2012). Visible Learning for Teachers: Maximizing Impact on Learning. Routledge.

- Zimmerman, B. J. (2002). "Becoming a self-regulated learner: An overview."

- Theory into Practice, 41(2), 64–70.

- Mischel, W., Shoda, Y., Rodriguez, M. I. (1989). "Delay of gratification in children." *Science*, 244(4907), 933–938.

- Willingham, D. T. (2009). *Why Don't Students Like School?* Jossey-Bass.

- Schmuck, R. A., Schmuck, P. A. (2001). *Group Processes in the Classroom* (8th ed.). McGraw Hill.

- Hess, F. M., McShane, M. Q. (2018). *Educational Entrepreneurship Today.* Harvard Education Press.

- Martinez, M., McGrath, D. (2014). Deeper Learning: How Eight Innovative Public Schools Are Transforming Education in the Twenty-First Century. New Press.

- Papert, S. (1980). Mindstorms: Children, Computers, and Powerful Ideas. Basic Books.

- Jensen, E. (2008). Brain-Based Learning: The New Science of Teaching and Training (2nd ed.). Corwin Press.

- Mayer, R. E., Moreno, R. (2003). "Nine ways to reduce cognitive load in multimedia learning." *Educational Psychologist*, 38(1), 43–52.

- Clark, R. C., Mayer, R. E. (2016). E-learning and the Science of Instruction: Proven Guidelines for Consumers and Designers of Multimedia Learning (4th ed.). Wiley.

- Rosenshine, B. (2012). "Principles of instruction: Research-based strategies that all teachers should know." *American Educator*, 36(1), 12–19.

- Mason, B. J., Bruning, R. (2001). "Providing feedback in computer-based instruction: What the research tells us." *Center for Instructional Innovation*, University of Nebraska.

- Veerman, A., Andriessen, J. (2010). "Arguing to learn." In K. Sawyer (Ed.), *The Cambridge Handbook of the Learning Sciences* (pp. 443–459). Cambridge University Press.

- Loveless, T., Coughlan, S. (2020). Between the State and the Schoolhouse: Understanding the Failure of Common Core. Harvard Education Press.

- Kuhn, D. (2005). "Education for thinking." *Harvard Educational Review*, 75(3), 397–410.

- Roediger, H. L., Putnam, A. L., Smith, M. A. (2011). "Ten benefits of testing and their applications to educational practice." *Psychology of Learning and Motivation*, 55, 1–36.

- Collins, A., Halverson, R. (2018). Rethinking Education in the Age of Technology: The Digital Revolution and Schooling in America (2nd ed.). Teachers College Press.

- Spencer, J., & Juliani, A. J. (2017). Empower: What Happens When Students Own Their Learning. IMpress Books.

- Lillard, A. S. (2013). *Montessori: The Science Behind the Genius* (2nd ed.). Oxford University Press.

- Howard-Jones, P. (2014). Neuroscience and Education: A Review of Educational Interventions and Approaches Informed by Neuroscience. Education Endowment Foundation.

- Brown, S., & Vaughan, C. (2009). Play: How It Shapes the Brain, Opens the Imagination, and Invigorates the Soul. Avery.

- Giedd, J. N. (2008). "The teen brain: Insights from neuroimaging." *Journal of Adolescent Health*, 42(4), 335–343.

- Galván, A. (2014). "Insights about adolescent behavior, plasticity, and policy from neuroscience research." *Neuron*, 83(2), 262–265.

- Lillard, A. S., Lerner, M. D., Hopkins, E. J., Dore, R. A., Smith, E. D., Palmquist, C. M. (2013). "The impact of pretend play on children's development: A review of the evidence." *Psychological Bulletin*, 139(1), 1–34.

- Hart, B., Risley, T. R. (1995). Meaningful Differences in the Everyday Experience of Young American Children. Paul H Brookes Publishing.

- Tudge, J. R. H., Doucet, F. (2004). "Early mathematical experiences: Observing young black and white children's everyday activities." *Early Childhood Research Quarterly*, 19(1), 21–39.

- Eberle, J. (2010). "Serious play." *American Journal of Play*, 2(4), 215–237.

- Goswami, U. (2008). Cognitive Development: The Learning Brain. Psychology Press.

- Sousa, D. A. (2011). *How the Gifted Brain Learns* (2nd ed.). Corwin Press.

- Lindquist, K. A., Barrett, L. F. (2012). "A functional architecture of the human brain: Emerging insights from the science of emotion." *Trends in Cognitive Sciences*, 16(11), 533–540.

- Noble, K. G., Tottenham, N., Casey, B. J. (2005). "Neuroscience perspectives on disparities in school readiness and cognitive achievement." *Future of Children*, 15(1), 71–89.

- van Merriënboer, J. J. G., Sweller, J. (2005). "Cognitive load theory and complex learning: Recent developments and future directions." *Educational Psychology Review*, 17(2), 147–177.

- McClelland, M. M., Tominey, S. L., Schmitt, S. A., Duncan, R. (2017). *SEL Interventions in Early Childhood.* Guilford Press.

- Goleman, D. (2006). Social Intelligence: The New Science of Human Relationships. Bantam.

- Shonkoff, J. P., Phillips, D. A. (Eds.). (2000). From Neurons to Neighborhoods: The Science of Early Childhood Development. National Academies Press.

- OECD. (2007). Understanding the Brain: The Birth of a Learning Science. OECD Publishing.

- Zull, J. E. (2002). The Art of Changing the Brain: Enriching Teaching by Exploring the Biology of Learning. Stylus Publishing.

- James, W. (1899). Talks to Teachers on Psychology and to Students on Some of Life's Ideals. Henry Holt & Co.

- Martinez, M. (2010). Learning and Cognition: The Design of the Mind. Pearson.

- Kolb, D. A. (1984).

- Experiential Learning: Experience as the Source of Learning and Development. Prentice Hall.

- Posner, M. I., Rothbart, M. K. (2009). "Toward a physical basis of attention and self-regulation." *Physics of Life Reviews*, 6(2), 103–120.

- Fuchs, L. S., Fuchs, D., Compton, D. L. (2004). "Monitoring early reading development in first grade: Word

identification fluency versus nonsense word fluency."
Exceptional Children, 71(1), 7–21.

- Kirschner, P. A., Hendrick, C. (2020). How Learning
Happens: Seminal Works in Educational Psychology and
What They Mean in Practice. Routledge.

- Moshman, D. (2011). Adolescent Rationality and
Development: Cognition, Morality, and Identity (3rd ed.).
Psychology Press.

- Edelman, G. M. (1992). Bright Air, Brilliant Fire: On the
Matter of the Mind. Basic Books.

- Tomasello, M. (2019). *Becoming Human: A Theory of
Ontogeny.* Harvard University Press.

- Howard-Jones, P. (2010). Introducing Neuroeducational
Research: Neuroscience, Education and the Brain from
Contexts to Practice. Routledge.

- Taylor, C. (2009). The Neuroscience of Human
Relationships: Attachment and the Developing Social Brain.
Norton & Company.

- Mercer, N. (2013). Exploring Talk in School: Inspired by the
Work of Douglas Barnes. SAGE Publications.

- Clark, R. E., Kirschner, P. A., Sweller, J. (2012). "Putting
students on the path to learning: The case for fully guided
instruction." *American Educator*, 36(1), 6–11.

- Claxton, G. (2008). What's the Point of School?
Rediscovering the Heart of Education. Oneworld
Publications.

- de Bruin, A. B. H., Dunlosky, J. (2020). "Monitoring and
regulation of learning: How metacognition helps, and why it

sometimes doesn't." *Educational Psychology Review*, 32(1), 1–14.

- Evans, J. S. B. T. (2011). *Thinking Twice: Two Minds in One Brain.* Oxford University Press.

- Noë, A. (2009). Out of Our Heads: Why You Are Not Your Brain, and Other Lessons from the Biology of Consciousness. Hill and Wang.

- Gopnik, A. (2009). The Philosophical Baby: What Children's Minds Tell Us About Truth, Love, and the Meaning of Life. Farrar, Straus and Giroux.

- Nokes-Malach, T. J., Richey, J. E., Gadgil, S. (2012). "When is it better to learn together? Insights from research on collaborative learning." *Educational Psychology Review*, 24(4), 629–645.

- Hasson, U., Ghazanfar, A. A., Galantucci, B., Garrod, S., Keysers, C. (2012). "Brain-to-brain coupling: A mechanism for creating and sharing a social world." *Trends in Cognitive Sciences*, 16(2), 114–121.

- Durlak, J. A., et al. (2011). "The Impact of Enhancing Students' Social and Emotional Learning: A Meta-Analysis of School-Based Universal Interventions." *Child Development*, 82(1), 405–432.

- Brown, P. C., Roediger III, H. L., & McDaniel, M. A. (2014). *Make It Stick: The Science of Successful Learning.* Belknap Press.

- Immordino-Yang, M. H., & Damasio, A. (2007). "We Feel, Therefore We Learn: The Relevance of Affective and Social Neuroscience to Education." *Mind, Brain, and Education*, 1(1), 3–10.

REFERENCES

- Bransford, J. D., Brown, A. L., & Cocking, R. R. (2000). *How People Learn: Brain, Mind, Experience, and School.* National Academy Press.

TEACH THE BRAIN